160

Easy French

Phrases

A Pocket Size Phrase Book for Travel

By

Fluency Pro

Disclaimer

1600+ Easy French Phrases
First Edition: March 11, 2023
Copyright © 2023 Caliber Brands Inc.
Cover images licensed through Shutterstock.

Table of Contents

INTRODUCTION

Welcome! This book includes common phrases that will be very beneficial while traveling to French-speaking countries, as they will assist you in conversing with people and carrying out day-to-day duties like as dining out and asking for directions when you are in those countries. This book will not only assist you in interpreting regional signage, but it also has the potential to broaden your understanding of French culture in general.

French is spoken in many parts of the world as a first or second language. It is recognized as an official language in a total of 29 countries, including France, Canada, Switzerland, Belgium, Haiti, and a number of countries in Africa. The total number of French speakers worldwide is estimated to be around 300 million, with approximately 76 million of them being native speakers. The majority of French speakers live in Africa, with countries such as Democratic Republic of the Congo, Cameroon, and Côte d'Ivoire having large numbers of French speakers. Other countries with significant numbers of French speakers include Canada, Belgium, and Switzerland.

French is an essential language in a wide variety of domains, including commerce, diplomatic work, and international relations. Being able to speak French fluently can make you a more competitive candidate for jobs with multinational companies and organizations. Furthermore, France is home to many large and influential companies in various industries, and being able to communicate effectively with French-speaking colleagues or clients can give you a significant advantage.

Learning French can make travel more enjoyable and immersive, as French is widely spoken around the world. If you visit France or other

French-speaking countries, you can easily navigate the local culture, read signs, order food, and interact with locals in their native language. Additionally, French-speaking countries offer a wide range of cultural and natural attractions that you can fully appreciate if you can communicate with locals.

French culture has made significant contributions to art, music, literature, philosophy, and cuisine. By learning French, you can better appreciate and understand these contributions, as well as the history and traditions of French-speaking countries. You can also discover French-speaking artists and intellectuals who have influenced global culture.

Learning French will help you connect with people from all walks of life and broaden your horizons. Additionally, French is widely studied in universities around the world, and knowing French can deepen your understanding of subjects taught in French, such as literature, history, and philosophy.

French-language media offers a unique perspective on global events and cultural trends. You can read French newspapers, magazines, and websites, and watch French films and TV shows to stay informed and entertained. In addition, picking up a second language can help you to pick up a third or even a fourth. This is because learning a new language helps develop various cognitive and linguistic skills, such as memory, attention, and grammar.

How This Book Is Organized

In this book, you will find over 1600 common French phrases organized by usage or situation.

Each entry includes the phrase in English, as well as its translation into French and a phonetic description written in a standard format. You can use the phonetic transcription to compare printed French words to sounds you are already familiar with if you want to get an idea of how

French words sound when spoken. Dashes have been utilized throughout each translation in order to create syllables. Capital letters draw attention to the stressed syllables that make up a phrase.

Vowels

French vowels are an essential part of learning the French language. French has a total of 13 vowel sounds, which can be pronounced in various ways depending on the word and context. In French, the pronunciation of vowels is crucial for conveying meaning, as two words can have different meanings based on their pronunciation.

The French letter "A" is pronounced as "ah" in "father" or "car". It is a very open vowel sound that is pronounced by opening the mouth wide. The letter "E" in French can be pronounced as "eh" in "red" or "ay" in "day", depending on the word. The French letter "I" is pronounced as "ee" in "bee". This vowel sound is produced by stretching the lips apart and raising the tongue to the front of the mouth.

The French letter "O" is pronounced as "oh" in "go". This vowel sound is similar to the English "o" sound, but the lips are rounded more. Finally, the French letter "U" is pronounced by rounding the lips and making a sound similar to "ee" in "bee", but with the tongue in the back of the mouth. This is a unique sound that is not found in English.

It is also important to note that French vowels can have accents, which can change their pronunciation. For example, the letter "é" is pronounced as "ay" in "day", while the letter "è" is pronounced as "eh" in "red". The accents in French also indicate stress and intonation patterns in words, which can affect the meaning of a sentence.

Learning proper pronunciation of French vowels takes practice and listening to native speakers. Listening to French music, watching

French films and TV shows, and practicing speaking with native speakers can also help improve your pronunciation of French vowels.

Consonants

French consonants are an important part of learning the French language. In French, consonants are pronounced differently from English consonants. It's essential to learn how to pronounce them correctly to communicate effectively in French.

The French letter "B" is pronounced as "b" in "baby". It is a voiced consonant, which means that the vocal cords vibrate when making the sound. The letter "C" in French is pronounced as "s" when followed by an "e", "i", or "y", and as "k" in all other cases. The French letter "D" is pronounced as "d" in "dog", similar to the English pronunciation. The letter "F" is pronounced as "f" in "four", also similar to the English pronunciation.

The French letter "G" is pronounced as "zh" (like the "s" in "pleasure") when followed by an "e", "i", or "y", and as "g" in all other cases. The letter "H" in French is generally not pronounced, except in certain loan words and expressions. The French letter "J" is pronounced as "zh" (like the "s" in "pleasure"). It is a voiced consonant, similar to the sound made in "measure."

The letter "K" in French is pronounced as "k" in all cases, like the English pronunciation. The letter "L" is pronounced as "l" in "love". The letter "M" is pronounced as "m" in "mother". The letter "N" is pronounced as "n" in "no". The letter "P" is pronounced as "p" in "pen". The letter "Q" in French is always followed by a "u" and pronounced as "k".

The French letter "R" is pronounced with a distinctive trilled or rolled "r" sound in the back of the throat. It is one of the most challenging consonant sounds to learn for English speakers. The letter "S" is pronounced as "s" in "sun", similar to the English pronunciation. The letter "T" is pronounced as "t" in "time", also similar to the English pronunciation. The letter "V" is pronounced as "v" in "very". The letter "W" is not a native French sound, but used in some loan words and expressions. The letter "X" is pronounced as "ks" in all cases. The letter "Y" is pronounced as "ee-grek" and used primarily as a vowel in French. Finally, the letter "Z" is pronounced as "z" in "zoo".

Stressors and Intonation

Stressors and intonation are essential elements of French pronunciation that can affect the meaning of words and phrases. French is a syllable-timed language, which means that each syllable takes approximately the same amount of time to pronounce. This is different from English, which is a stress-timed language, where stressed syllables are emphasized and take longer to pronounce than unstressed syllables.

Stress in French is primarily used to distinguish between different grammatical forms of the same word. For example, the word "présent" can be pronounced with stress on the first syllable ("pré-sent") to mean "gift," or with stress on the second syllable ("pré-sent") to mean "present" as in "right now."

Intonation in French can be used to indicate a question or a statement. A rising intonation at the end of a sentence typically indicates a question, while a falling intonation indicates a statement.

French also uses intonation to convey emotion or emphasis. A speaker may use a rising or falling intonation to express surprise, enthusiasm, or disappointment, among other emotions.

Liaison is another important element of French pronunciation. It involves linking the final consonant of one word to the beginning vowel of the next word in a phrase, creating a seamless flow of sound. For example, "les amis" (the friends) is pronounced with a liaison between the "s" in "les" and the "a" in "amis," resulting in the sound "lezamis."

Enunciation is also important in French pronunciation, particularly when it comes to vowel sounds. Each vowel sound should be pronounced clearly and distinctly, as some words can have different meanings depending on the vowel sound used. For example, the word "été" (summer) is pronounced with an open "e" sound, while "été" (been) is pronounced with a closed "e" sound.

Overall, stressors and intonation play an important role in French pronunciation, conveying meaning, emotion, and emphasis. As with other aspects of French pronunciation, practice and exposure to native speakers are key to developing a good ear for these elements of the language.

ORDERING FOOD

Can I see the menu, please?
Puis-je voir le menu, s'il vous plaît ?
POUIS-JUH vwah luh meh-NUH, SEEL VOUS PLAIT?

What do you recommend?
Qu'est-ce que vous recommandez ?
KESS-kuh voo REH-koh-mahn-DAY?

Could you tell me about the specials of the day?
Pourriez-vous me parler des plats du jour ?
POOR-ree-ay voo muh pahr-LAY day PLOH duh ZHOOR?

I would like to order the (dish name), please.
Je voudrais commander le (nom du plat), s'il vous plaît.
JUH voo-DREH koh-mahn-DAY luh (nom duh plah), SEEL VOO PLAIT.

Can I have (side item) with that?
Puis-je avoir (nom de l'accompagnement) avec ça ?
POUIS-JUH ah-VOAR (nom duh l'ah-kohm-pah-NYEH-mahn) ah-VEK sah?

Is it possible to make that (dish name) spicy/mild?
Est-il possible de rendre ce plat épicé/doux ?
ES-TEEL poh-SEE-bluh duh RONDR suh plah eh-PEE-say/doo?

How long will it take for our order to be ready?
Combien de temps faut-il pour préparer notre commande ?
KOM-bee-ehn duh TAHN pohr pruh-PAH-ray noh-truh koh-mahn-DUH?

Can we get separate checks, please?
Pouvons-nous avoir des additions séparées, s'il vous plaît ?
POO-vohn NOOZ av-WAHR day ZAH-dee-syoh-NAY, SEEL VOO PLAIT?

I'd like to pay by credit card.
Je voudrais payer par carte de crédit.
Juh voo-DREH pay-AY par KART duh KREH-DEE.

Can you please add a 15% tip to the bill?
Pouvez-vous ajouter un pourboire de 15% à l'addition, s'il vous plaît ?
POO-vay voo ah-ZHOOT-AY uhn poor-BWAHR duh KANZ pour-sah duh l'ah-dee-SYOHN, SEEL VOO PLAIT?

Excuse me, there's a mistake on my bill.
Excusez-moi, il y a une erreur sur ma facture.
EX-kooz-AY MWAH, eel YAH uh-NEH-RUHR sur ma fahk-TOOR.

We'll split the bill evenly.
Nous allons diviser l'addition en parts égales.
NOOZ a-LOHN deev-EE-zee LAD-dee-SYOHN ahn PAR-tih-GAHL.

Could I get a receipt, please?
Puis-je avoir un reçu, s'il vous plaît ?
POUIS-JUH ah-VOAR uhn ruh-SUH, SEEL VOO PLAIT?

I think we're ready for the check now.
Je pense que nous sommes prêts à payer maintenant.
JUH PONSS kuh noo SOM prays ah PAY-AY mahn-TUH.

Can we order dessert?
Pouvons-nous commander un dessert ?
POO-vohn NOOZ koh-mahn-DAY uhn day-ZAIR?

I have a food allergy, could you tell me which dishes I should avoid?
J'ai une allergie alimentaire, pourriez-vous me dire quels plats je dois éviter ?
JAY ewn ah-luhr-jee ah-LEE-mahn-TAIR, poor-REE-voo muh DEER kell plah zhuh DO-eez eh-VEE-tay?

Could we have the bill now, please?
Pouvons-nous avoir l'addition maintenant, s'il vous plaît ?
POO-vohn NOOZ av-WAHR LAD-dee-SYOHN mahnt-nahn, SEEL VOO PLAIT?

How much is the (dish name)?
Combien coûte le (nom du plat) ?
KOM-bee-ehn koot luh (nom duh plah)?

Do you have a kids' menu?
Avez-vous un menu pour enfants ?
AH-vay-VOO uhn meh-NUU pohr zan-FAHN?

I would like to place a takeout order, please.
Je voudrais passer une commande à emporter, s'il vous plaît.
Juh voo-DREH pah-SAY uhn koh-mahn-DUH ah-TOOM-bay, SEEL VOO PLAIT.

BUYING TRAVEL TICKETS

Hello, can I please have a ticket to [destination]?
Bonjour, puis-je avoir un billet pour [destination], s'il vous plaît?
Bohn-ZHOOR, pwee-zhah-vwar un bee-YAY poo(r) [destination], seel voo pleh?

I'd like to purchase a round-trip ticket to [destination].
Je voudrais acheter un billet aller-retour pour [destination].
Zhuh voo-dreh ah-shee-tey un bee-YAY ah-lay-ruh-toor poo(r) [destination].

How much does a one-way ticket to [destination] cost?
Combien coûte un billet aller simple pour [destination]?
Kohm-bee-ahn koot uh bee-YAY ah-layr sah(n)pl pour [destination]?

Are there any discounts available for students/seniors/military?
Y a-t-il des réductions disponibles pour les étudiants / les personnes âgées / les militaires?
Ee-yah-TEEL day rey-dook-see-yoh(n) ah-vay-lah(bl) poo(r) lay-zeh-too-dyah(n) / lay pair-sohn-ah-zhay / lay mee-lee-tair?

Can I reserve a seat on the train to [destination]?
Puis-je réserver une place dans le train pour [destination]?
Pwee-jhuh reh-zehr-vay ewn plahs dahn luh trahn poo(r) [destination]?

What time does the next train to [destination] depart?
À quelle heure part le prochain train pour [destination]?
Ah kell uhr pahr luh proh-shahn trahn poo(r) [destination]?

How long does the journey take to get to [destination]?
Combien de temps dure le voyage pour arriver à [destination]?
Kohm-bee-ahn duhr luh voy-ahzh poor ah-ree-vay ah [destination]?

Can I pay with a credit card?
Puis-je payer avec une carte de crédit?
Pwee-jhuh pay-ay ah-vehk ewn kahrt duh kray-dee?

Is there a train that goes directly to [destination]?
Y a-t-il un train direct pour [destination]?
Ee-yah-TEEL uh(n) trahn dee-rekt poor [destination]?

Do I need to validate my ticket before boarding the train?
Dois-je valider mon billet avant de monter dans le train?
Dwahzh vah-lee-day mohn bee-YAY ah-vah(n) duh mohn-tay dahn luh trahn?

Hi, can I please purchase a one-way ticket to [destination]?
Bonjour, puis-je acheter un billet aller simple pour [destination], s'il vous plaît?
Bonjour, PUHJ zheh ach-uh-TEH uhn bee-YEH al-LEHR SEMP-leu pour [destination], seel voo PLEH?

What's the earliest flight to [destination] that you have available?
Quel est le premier vol pour [destination] que vous avez disponible?
KELL eh luh pre-mee-AYR vohl pour [destination] kuh voo zah-VEH zavaykuh-dzee-PON-ee-bluh?

How much is a round-trip ticket to [destination]?
Combien coûte un billet aller-retour pour [destination]?
KOM-byehn koot uhn bee-YEH al-lehr-TOOR pour [destination]?

Can I check in my bags here at the airport?
Puis-je enregistrer mes bagages ici à l'aéroport?
PUHJ ahn-grees-TRAY may ba-GAJZ ee-see ah-low-roh por [destination]?

Are there any direct flights to [destination]?
Y a-t-il des vols directs pour [destination]?
EE ah-TEEL day-rekt por [destination]?

How long is the layover if I take a connecting flight?
Combien de temps dure l'escale si je prends un vol de correspondance?
KOM-byehn duhr luh ess-kahl see zhuh prahn uhn vohl duh kor-respond-ahns?

Can I get a refund if I need to cancel my flight?
Puis-je obtenir un remboursement si j'ai besoin d'annuler mon vol?
PUHJ ohb-teh-neer uhn rehm-BOORSS-mahn see zheh be-SWAHN dah-nyoo-lay mohn vohl?

What's the maximum weight for carry-on luggage?
Quel est le poids maximal pour les bagages en cabine?
KELL eh luh pwa mah-ksi-mahl poor ley ba-GAJZ ahn kah-BEEN?

Do I need to show ID to purchase a ticket?
Dois-je présenter une pièce d'identité pour acheter un billet?
DWASJ pray-zahn-tehr uhn pee-S dahn-tee-TEH poor ah-shuh-teh uhn bee-YEH?

Can I choose my seat on the plane?
Puis-je choisir mon siège dans l'avion?
PUHJ sho-ee-ZEER mohn seezh dan lav-yohn?

Hello, can I please purchase a ticket to [destination]?
Bonjour, puis-je acheter un billet pour [destination], s'il vous plaît?
Bohn-ZHOOR, pwee-zhuh ah-shuh-teh uh bee-YEH pohr [destination], seel voo play?

Are there any buses that go directly to [destination]?
Y a-t-il des bus qui vont directement à [destination]?
Ee ah-TEEL day boos kee vawn dee-rek-teh-mahn ah [destination]?

What time does the next bus to [destination] depart?
À quelle heure part le prochain bus pour [destination]?
Ah kell uhr pahr luh proh-SHEN boos pour [destination]?

How long does the journey take to get to [destination]?
Combien de temps dure le voyage pour arriver à [destination]?
Kohm-BYAN duhr luh voy-ahzh poor ah-ree-VAY ah [destination]?

Can I bring a pet on the bus with me?
Puis-je amener un animal de compagnie dans le bus avec moi?
Pwee-zhuh ah-muh-neh run ah-nee-mahl duh kohm-pahn-yee dahn luh boos ah-vehk mwa?

How much does a one-way ticket to [destination] cost?
Combien coûte un billet aller simple pour [destination]?
kohm-BYAN koot un bee-YEH tah-layr sahm-PLUH poor [destination]?

Can I purchase a ticket online?
Puis-je acheter un billet en ligne?
Pwee-zhuh ah-shuh-teh un bee-YEH ahn leen?

Is there a discount for purchasing a round-trip ticket?
Y a-t-il une réduction pour l'achat d'un billet aller-retour?
Ee ah-TEEL ewn ray-dook-see-yohn poor lah-sha duh un bee-YEH tah-layr-ruh-tour?

Can I pay for my ticket with cash?
Puis-je payer mon billet en espèces?
Pwee-zhuh pay-eh mohn bee-YEH ahn ess-pehss?

Do I need to print out my ticket before boarding the bus?
Dois-je imprimer mon billet avant de monter dans le bus?
Dwahzh ahn-pree-may mohn bee-YEH ah-vahnt duh mohn-tay dahn luh boos?

Hi, can I please get a ride to [destination]?
Bonjour, puis-je avoir une course pour [destination], s'il vous plaît?
Bohn-JOOR, pweeZH ah-VWAHR oon KORS poor [destination], seel voo play?

How much will it cost to get to [destination]?
Combien cela coûtera-t-il pour aller à [destination]?
Kohm-BYAN suh-LA koo-TUH-rah-teel poor ah-LAY ah [destination]?

Can I pay with a credit card?
Puis-je payer avec une carte de crédit?
PweeZH pey-AY ah-VEK oon KART duh kray-DEE?

Is there a flat rate for trips to the airport?
Y a-t-il un tarif fixe pour les trajets vers l'aéroport?
Ee ah-TEEL uhN tah-REEF feeks poor lay trah-JAY vairz lay-air-oh-POR?

How long will it take to get to [destination]?
Combien de temps cela prendra-t-il pour arriver à [destination]?
Kohm-BYAN duh tahN suh-LA prohn-DRAY-teel poor ah-ree-VAY ah [destination]?

Can I share a taxi with someone else to save money?
Puis-je partager un taxi avec quelqu'un d'autre pour économiser de l'argent?
PweeZH par-tah-ZHAY uhN tahk-SEE ah-VEK kell-KUHN dahtr poor ay-koh-noh-MEE-zay duh lahR-zhahn?

Do you have child car seats available?
Avez-vous des sièges d'auto pour enfants disponibles?
Ah-VAY voo day seej doh-toh poor an-FAHN dis-poh-NEEBL?

Is there a fee for bringing luggage?
Y a-t-il des frais pour les bagages?
Ee ah-TEEL day fray poor lay bah-GAZH?

Do I need to tip the driver?
Dois-je donner un pourboire au chauffeur?
Dwahzh doh-NAY uh poor-BWAHR oh shoh-foor?

EMERGENCY SITUATIONS

I need help.
J'ai besoin d'aide.
ZHAY buh-ZWAH d'EYD.

I need immediate assistance.
J'ai besoin d'une assistance immédiate.
ZHAY buh-ZWAH d'YUN ah-SEE-stahnts ee-MEH-dee-at.

Someone call an ambulance!
Quelqu'un appelle une ambulance !
KELL-kuhn ah-PELL oon ahm-BOO-lahns!

This is an emergency!
C'est une urgence!
SAY tewn OOR-jawns!

Please help me!
S'il vous plaît, aidez-moi !
SEEL voo PLEH, ed-AY mwa!

I'm in trouble!
J'ai des ennuis !
ZHAY day zeh-NU-ee!

I'm in danger!
Je suis en danger !
ZHuh swee ahn don-ZHAY!

I'm hurt!
Je suis blessé(e) !
ZHuh swee bles-AY(e)!

I'm injured!
Je suis blessé(e)!
Zhuh swee bles-AY(e)!

I can't breathe!
Je ne peux pas respirer!
Zhuh nuh puh pah reh-speh-RAY!

Please call for help!
S'il vous plaît, appelez à l'aide!
Seel voo pleh, ah-PELL-eh ah lehd!

Somebody please help me!
Quelqu'un s'il vous plaît, aidez-moi!
Kell-kuhn seel voo pleh, ed-AY-mwa!

I'm having a heart attack!
Je suis en train de faire une crise cardiaque!
Zhuh swee ahn trawn duh fair oon kreez car-dee-YACK!

I'm having a stroke!
Je suis en train d'avoir une attaque cérébrale!
Zhuh swee ahn trawn dah-vwahr oon ah-TAK say-ray-bral!

I'm having an allergic reaction!
Je suis en train de faire une réaction allergique!
Zhuh swee ahn trawn duh fair oon ray-ak-see-YAWN ah-lair-zheek!

I'm having a seizure!
Je fais une crise d'épilepsie!
Zhuh fay oon kreez day-pee-LEP-see!

I'm choking!
Je m'étouffe!
Zhuh may-TOOF!

I'm drowning!
Je suis en train de me noyer!
Zhuh swee ahn trawn duh muh nwah-YAY!

My house is on fire!
Ma maison est en feu!
MAH meh-ZON eh-TAHN fuh!

My car crashed!
Ma voiture s'est crashée!
MAH vwah-TUHR sest krah-SHAY!

My child is missing!
Mon enfant est disparu!
MOHn ahn-FAHN eh dee-spah-ROO!

My loved one is in danger!
Mon être cher est en danger!
MOHN eh-truh SHEHr eh-TAHN dahn-JAY!

I need medical attention!
J'ai besoin d'attention médicale!
ZHAY buh-ZWAH dahn-TAHN-syawn may-dee-KAHL!

I'm trapped!
Je suis piégé(e)!
Zhuh swee pyeh-ZHAY!

I'm lost!
Je suis perdu(e)!
Zhuh swee pehr-DUH!

I'm stranded!
Je suis bloqué(e)!
Zhuh swee bloh-KAY!

My pet needs urgent medical care!
Mon animal de compagnie a besoin de soins médicaux urgents!
MOHN ah-nee-mahl duh kohn-pahn-yeh ah buh-ZWAH duh swahn may-dee-KOH urzhahn!

Call the police!
Appelez la police!
Ah-peh-LAY lah poh-LEES!

Call an ambulance!
Appelez une ambulance!
Ah-peh-LAY ewn ahm-BOOLAHNS!

Call the fire department!
Appelez les pompiers!
Ah-peh-LAY lay pohm-PYAY!

Where is the nearest hospital/police station/fire station?
Où se trouve l'hôpital/la station de police/la caserne de pompiers la plus proche ?
Ooh suh troov lop-EE-tahl/la stah-see-ohn duh poh-lees/la kah-sairn duh pohm-pee-ay lah ploo prosh

TECH SUPPORT

I am having problems with my computer.
J'ai des problèmes avec mon ordinateur.
ZHAY day pro-BLEM ah-vehk mawn or-dee-nuh-TUHR.

My internet connection is slow.
Ma connexion internet est lente.
MAH kohn-ehk-see-YAWN ahn-tern-EH eh len-tuh.

I forgot my password.
J'ai oublié mon mot de passe.
ZHAY ooh-blee-AY mawn moh duh PAHS.

The website is not loading.
Le site web ne se charge pas.
Luh SEET web nuh suh shahrzh pah.

My email account is not working.
Mon compte email ne fonctionne pas.
Mawn kohnt ee-mehl nuh fawnk-SYUN pah.

The printer is not printing.
L'imprimante ne fonctionne pas.
Lim-pree-MAWNT nuh fawnk-SYUN pah.

My computer crashed.
Mon ordinateur a planté.
Mawn or-dee-nuh-TUHR ah plawn-TAY.

The software is not working.
Le logiciel ne fonctionne pas.
Luh loh-gee-SEE-ehl nuh fawnk-SYUN pah.

I am receiving error messages.
Je reçois des messages d'erreur.
Zhuh ruh-SWAH day mess-AJ duh-RUHR.

The computer is frozen.
L'ordinateur est gelé.
LOR-dee-nuh-TUHR eh zhuh-LAY.

My keyboard is not working.
Mon clavier ne fonctionne pas.
Mawn klah-VYAY nuh fawnk-SYUN pah.

I cannot access my files.
Je ne peux pas accéder à mes fichiers.
Zhuh nuh puh pah ak-seh-DAY ah may fee-syay.

The computer is making strange noises.
L'ordinateur émet des bruits étranges.
LOR-dee-nuh-TUHR ay-MAY day brwee ay-trawnzh.

I need to update my software.
Je dois mettre à jour mon logiciel.
Zhuh dwah maitr ah zhoor mawn loh-gi-SEE-ehl.

My computer is infected with a virus.
Mon ordinateur est infecté par un virus.
Mawn or-dee-nuh-TUHR eh tahn-FEK-tay pahr uh VEE-rus.

The mouse is not working.
La souris ne fonctionne pas.
La soo-REE nuh fawnk-SYUN pah.

I accidentally deleted important files.
J'ai supprimé accidentellement des fichiers importants.
*ZHAY soo-pree-MAY ak-see-dawn-tell-MUHNT day fee-syay
im-por-TAHNT.*

I need help setting up my new device.
J'ai besoin d'aide pour installer mon nouvel appareil.
ZHAY buh-ZWAH dahyd poor ahn-stah-LAY mawn noo-VEL ah-puh-RAY.

The screen is black.
L'écran est noir.
LAY-krahn eh nwahr.

I accidentally spilled water on my laptop.
J'ai renversé accidentellement de l'eau sur mon ordinateur portable.
ZHAY rahn-ver-SAY ak-see-dawn-tell-MUHNT duh loh sooR mawn
or-dee-nuh-TUHR pohr-tahbl.

The battery is not charging.
La batterie ne se charge pas.
La ba-teh-REE nuh suh shahrzh pah.

My computer is overheating.
Mon ordinateur surchauffe.
Mawn or-dee-nuh-TUHR sur-shohf.

The sound is not working.
Le son ne fonctionne pas.
Luh sohn nuh fawnk-SYUN pah.

I accidentally uninstalled an important program.
J'ai désinstallé accidentellement un programme important.
ZHAY day-san-stal-AY ak-see-dawn-tell-MUHNT uh proh-GRAMM
im-por-TAHNT.

The internet is not connecting.
Internet ne se connecte pas.
Ahn-tair-NEHT nuh suh kohn-nekt pah.

I need to recover deleted files.
J'ai besoin de récupérer des fichiers supprimés.
ZHAY buh-ZWAH duh reh-koo-pay-RAY day fee-syay soo-pree-MAY.

My printer is not printing.
Mon imprimante n'imprime pas.
Mawn ahm-pree-MAHN nuhm-preem pah.

I can't access my email.
Je ne peux pas accéder à mon courrier électronique.
Zhuh nuh puh pah ak-seh-DAY ah mawn koor-YAY eh-lehk-troh-NEEK.

I forgot my password.
J'ai oublié mon mot de passe.
ZHAY oo-blee-AY mawn moh duh pahs.

The CD/DVD drive is not working.
Le lecteur CD/DVD ne fonctionne pas.
Luh lek-TUHR say-day-day-VEH/DAY-VAY-DAY nuh fawnk-SYUN pah.

I'm having trouble with my [device or software].
J'ai des problèmes avec mon [appareil/ logiciel].
ZHAY day proh-BLEM uh-vehk mawn [ah-puh-RAY/loh-gi-SEE-ehl].

Can you help me troubleshoot the issue?
Pouvez-vous m'aider à résoudre le problème ?
Poo-VAY voo meh-DAY ah reh-soo-druh luh proh-BLEM?

What should I do if my [device or software] isn't working properly?
Que dois-je faire si mon [appareil/ logiciel] ne fonctionne pas
correctement ?
*Kuh dwahzh fair si mawn [ah-puh-RAY/loh-gi-SEE-ehl] nuh fawnk-SYUN
pah koh-REHK-teh-mahn?*

I'm getting an error message. What does it mean?
Je reçois un message d'erreur. Qu'est-ce que ça veut dire ?
Zhuh ruh-SWAH uh mess-AJ duh-RUHR. KESS-kuh sah vuh deer?

How do I update my [device or software]?
Comment mettre à jour mon [appareil/ logiciel] ?
Kuh-MOHN met-truh ah ZHOOR mawn [ah-puh-RAY/loh-gi-SEE-ehl]?

Can you walk me through the steps to fix the problem?
Pouvez-vous me guider à travers les étapes pour résoudre le problème
?
*Poo-VAY voo muh gee-DAY ah trah-vair lay-TAP pohr reh-soo-druh luh
proh-BLEM?*

Do I need to bring my [device or software] in for repair?
Dois-je amener mon [appareil/ logiciel] pour réparation ?
*Dwahzh-juh ah-muh-NAY mawn [ah-puh-RAY/loh-gi-SEE-ehl] poor
reh-pah-rah-SEE-yohn?*

How long will the repair take?
Combien de temps prendra la réparation ?
Kohm-BYAN duh TAHN prahn-drah luh reh-pah-rah-SEE-yohn?

Is it possible to recover lost data from my [device or software]?
Est-il possible de récupérer les données perdues de mon [appareil/
logiciel] ?
*Eh-TEEL poh-SEE-bluh duh reh-koo-pay-RAY lay doh-NAY pehr-doo duh
mawn [ah-puh-RAY/loh-gi-SEE-ehl]?*

CASUAL CONVERSATION AND SMALL TALK

Hi, how are you doing today?
Salut, comment ça va aujourd'hui ?
SAH-LOO, koh-mah sah VA oh-zhoor-DWEE

Nice weather we're having, isn't it?
Il fait beau, n'est-ce pas ?
Eel FAY boh, nehss-pah

Have you been up to anything interesting lately?
Avez-vous fait quelque chose d'intéressant récemment ?
AH-veh VOO feh kelk CHOHZ dan-teh-re-SAHN reh-SEM-men

Did you catch the game last night?
Avez-vous regardé le match hier soir ?
AH-veh VOO ruh-gar-DEH luh mahsh ee-yehr SWAR

What do you like to do for fun?
Qu'est-ce que vous aimez faire pour vous amuser ?
KESS-kuh VOOZ EH-may fair poor vooz ah-moo-SAY

How's work/school going?
Comment ça se passe au travail/à l'école ?
Koh-mah sah suh PAHS oh trav-AY/ah luh-KOL

Have you been on any vacations recently?
Êtes-vous parti en vacances récemment ?
ET-voo par-TEE ah vah-KAHNS reh-sem-men

What's your favorite type of music/movie/TV show?
Quel est votre type de musique/film/émission de télévision préféré ?
KELL eh voh-truh TEEP duh moo-ZEEK/feel/em-mee-zee-yon duh teh-lee-vee-ZYON pray-fay-RAY

Do you have any pets?
Avez-vous des animaux de compagnie ?
AH-veh VOO day zan-ee-MOH duh kohm-pahn-YEE

Have you tried any new restaurants lately?
Avez-vous essayé de nouveaux restaurants récemment ?
AH-veh VOO eh-sah-YAY duh noo-VOH res-toh-RAHN reh-sem-men

How's your family doing?
Comment va votre famille ?
Koh-mah vah vo-truh fa-mee

What are your plans for the weekend?
Quels sont vos projets pour le week-end ?
KELL sohn vo pproh-JAY poor luh week-end

Do you like to read? What kind of books do you enjoy?
Aimez-vous lire ? Quel genre de livres préférez-vous ?
EH-may VOO leer? KELL zhawn-duhr duh leevr pray-feh-ray VOO

Have you seen any good movies lately?
Avez-vous vu des bons films récemment ?
AH-veh VOO voo day bohn feelm reh-sem-men

How long have you lived in this area?
Depuis combien de temps habitez-vous dans cette région ?
Deh-PWEE kohm-BYAN duh tah eh-bee-TAY VOO dahn set reh-ZYON

Have you been to any concerts recently?
Êtes-vous allé à des concerts récemment ?
ET-voo zah-lay ah day kohn-sehr reh-sem-men

Do you have any hobbies?
Avez-vous des hobbies ?
AH-veh VOO day zoh-bee

What's your favorite thing to do in your free time?
Quelle est votre activité préférée pendant votre temps libre ?
KELL eh vo-truh ahk-tee-vee-tay pray-fay-RAY pahn-dahn vo-truh tahN lee-bruh

Have you been following any interesting news stories lately?
Avez-vous suivi des histoires d'actualités intéressantes récemment ?
AH-veh VOO swee-vee day ZEE-stwahr dahk-tyoo-ah-lee-tay
ahN-teh-re-SAHNT reh-sem-men

Do you like to cook? What's your favorite dish to make?
Aimez-vous cuisiner ? Quel est votre plat préféré à faire ?
EH-may VOO kwee-zeen-AY? KELL eh vo-truh plah pray-fay-RAY ah
fair?

Do you enjoy exercising? What kind of workouts do you do?
Aimez-vous faire de l'exercice ? Quel genre d'entraînement faites-vous
?
EH-may VOO fair duh lex-ehr-SEES? KELL zhawn-duh on-tray-nuh-mohn
feh-TEH VOO

How do you like your coffee/tea?
Comment aimez-vous votre café/thé ?
Koh-mahn EH-may VOO vo-truh kah-FAY / tay

What's your favorite restaurant in town?
Quel est votre restaurant préféré en ville ?
KELL eh vo-truh reh-stoh-RAHN pray-fay-RAY ahn veel

Do you have any plans for the holidays?
Avez-vous des projets pour les vacances ?
AH-veh VOO day proh-JAY poor lay vah-KAHNS

Have you ever gone bungee jumping/skydiving/rock climbing?
Avez-vous déjà fait du saut à l'élastique/parachutisme/escalade ?
AH-veh VOO day-jah fay doo soh-tah-lay-steeck / pah-rah-shoo-TEEZM
/ ess-kah-LAHD

What's your favorite type of cuisine?
Quel est votre type de cuisine préféré ?
KELL eh vo-truh teep duh kwee-ZEEN pray-fay-RAY

Do you have any siblings? What are they like?
Avez-vous des frères et sœurs ? Comment sont-ils ?
AH-veh VOO day frair-AY eh suhr? koh-mahn sohn-teel

Have you read any good books lately?

Avez-vous lu de bons livres récemment ?

AH-veh VOO lew day bohn leev-reh reh-sem-men

Do you have any plans for the summer?

Avez-vous des projets pour l'été ?

AH-veh VOO day proh-JAY poor let-TAY

Hi, it's nice to finally meet you in person.
Salut, c'est sympa de te rencontrer enfin en personne.
SAH-LUH, say sohN-pah duh tuh rehn-kohn-treh ahn-FAHN ahN pehr-sohn.

So, tell me a bit about yourself. What do you like to do for fun?
Alors, raconte-moi un peu de toi. Qu'aimes-tu faire pour t'amuser ?
AH-LOR, rah-KOHNT-mwah uhN puh duh twa. KEHM tew fehr pour tah-mew-ZAY.

I love this restaurant! Have you been here before?
J'adore ce restaurant ! Tu y es déjà venue ?
ZHAD-OR suh rehs-toh-RAHN ! too ee eh deh-JAH veh-NU.

Can I get you something to drink? The wine here is supposed to be amazing.
Est-ce que je peux te servir quelque chose à boire ? Le vin ici est censé être incroyable.
EHSS kuh zhuh puh tuh sehr-VEER kelk shohz ah bwahr ? luh vaN ee-SEE eh suhN-sey eht ahN-kwah-YAHBL.

You look really nice tonight.
Tu es vraiment élégante ce soir.
Too eh vruh-mahN EH-ley-gahN suh swahr.

This place has a great atmosphere, don't you think?
Cet endroit a une atmosphère géniale, tu ne trouves pas ?
SET ahN-dwah ah ewn ah-toh-SFEHR zheh-NYAL, too nuh troov pah?

What do you do for work? I'm always interested in hearing about other people's jobs.
Que fais-tu dans la vie ? Je suis toujours intéressée par les métiers des autres.
Kuh feh-TU dahN lah vee ? zhuh swee too-jurz ahN-teh-ray-SEY pahr lay meh-TEEYR dehz ohtr.

I'm really enjoying our conversation so far.
Je prends vraiment plaisir à discuter avec toi.
Zhuh prohN vruh-mahN pleh-ZEER ah dee-skew-tey ah-VEK twa.

Would you like to split an appetizer? I hear the calamari is fantastic.
Veux-tu partager une entrée ? J'ai entendu dire que les calmars sont
fantastiques.
VUH-tu pahr-tah-ZHEYR ewn ahN-trey ? zheh-zah-ee ahN-dew DEER
kuh lay kahl-MAHR sohN fahN-tah-STEEK.

Have you traveled anywhere interesting lately?
As-tu voyagé quelque part de fascinant récemment ?
AH-stu vwah-YA-jey kelk pahr duh fah-si-NAHN rey-sah-MEH?

So, what are your hobbies? I'm always looking for new things to try.
Alors, quels sont tes passe-temps ? Je suis toujours à la recherche de
nouvelles choses à essayer.
AH-LOR, kuh sohN tay pahs-TAHN ? zhuh swee too-jurz ah lah
ruh-sherch duh noo-VEL shohz ah ess-AY-yey.

**I had a great time on our last date. I'm really looking forward to
tonight.**
J'ai passé un super moment lors de notre dernière rencontre. J'ai
vraiment hâte pour ce soir.
ZHAY pah-SAY uhN soo-PAIR moh-MAHN lohr duh nohtr dernyehr
ruhn-kohntr. zhay vruh-mahN aht pour suh swahr.

Do you prefer action movies or comedies?
Préfères-tu les films d'action ou les comédies ?
PREH-fehr too lay feelm dahk-see-YOHn oo lay koh-may-DEE?

What's your favorite type of cuisine?
Quel est ton type de cuisine préféré ?
KEL eh tohn teep duh kwee-ZEEN preh-fer-ey?

Have you read any good books or seen any good movies lately?
As-tu lu des bons livres ou vu des bons films récemment ?
AH-stu lew day bohN livr oo vew day bohN feelm rey-sah-MEH?

I really appreciate you taking the time to come out with me tonight.
Je suis vraiment reconnaissante que tu aies pris le temps de sortir avec moi ce soir.
Zhuh swee vruh-mahN ruh-koh-nay-SAHN kuh too EH pree luh tohN duh sor-TEER ah-VEK mwah suh swahr.

Have you ever tried sushi? There's a great sushi place down the street.
As-tu déjà essayé le sushi ? Il y a un super restaurant de sushi dans la rue.
AH-stu deh-JAH ess-AY-yey luh soo-SHEE ? eel ee-ah uhN soo-pair reh-stoh-RAHN duh soo-SHEE daN lah rew.

What's your favorite thing to do on a lazy Sunday?
Quelle est ta chose préférée à faire un dimanche tranquille ?
KEL eh ta shohz preh-fer-ey ah fehr uhN dee-MAHN-sh trahN-KEEL.

I'm really enjoying spending time with you.
J'apprécie vraiment passer du temps avec toi.
Zhah-preh-SEE vruh-mahN pah-SAY duh tohN ah-VEK twa.

Do you have any siblings?
As-tu des frères ou sœurs ?
AH-stu day frair oo suhr ?

Do you prefer coffee or tea?
Préférez-vous le café ou le thé ?
PREH-FEH-REH-VOO luh KA-FEH oo luh TAY?

I've always wanted to try skydiving. Have you?
J'ai toujours voulu essayer le parachutisme. Et vous ?
ZHAY too-jOOR voo-LOO eh-seh-YEH luh pah-rah-shoo-TEESM. eh VOO?

Your outfit looks great on you.
Votre tenue vous va très bien.
VOH-truh tuh-NOO voo vah TREH bee-EN.

What's your favorite hobby?
Quel est votre passe-temps préféré ?
KELL EH voh-truh pahs-TAHN preh-FEH-RAY?

This place has a really cozy atmosphere.
Cet endroit a une atmosphère vraiment confortable.
SET ahn-DROIT ah oon aht-moh-SFEHR vrè-mahng kohn-FOR-tahbl.

What kind of books do you like to read?
Quel genre de livres aimez-vous lire ?
KELL zhanr duh LEEVREH eh-MEH-voo leer?

Have you been to any concerts recently?
Êtes-vous allé à des concerts récemment ?
EH-tuh VOO ah-LAY ah day kon-SAIR ray-seh-mahn.

Your smile is contagious!
Votre sourire est contagieux !
VOH-truh soo-REER eh kohn-tah-zhee-UE.

I'm so glad we decided to go out tonight.
Je suis tellement content que nous ayons décidé de sortir ce soir.
ZHuh swee TEH-leh-mahn kohn-TAHN kuh noo-zeh-yohn day-see-day duh sohr-teer suh SWAHR.

Do you have any upcoming travel plans?
Avez-vous des projets de voyage à venir ?
AH-veh-VOO day proh-ZHEH duh voh-YAJ ah vuh-NEER?

SHOPPING AT A CLOTHING STORE

What is your return policy?
Quelle est votre politique de retour?
KELL eh VOH-truh poh-lee-SEEK duh ruh-TUR?

Do you have this item in a different color?
Avez-vous cet article dans une couleur différente?
AH-veh VOO set ahrt-EE-kl duhN oon kuh-LEWR DEE-fay-RAWT?

Can I try this on?
Puis-je l'essayer?
PWEEDZH leh-seh-EE-ay?

Where are your fitting rooms?
Où sont vos cabines d'essayage?
OO sohn voh KAH-been dess-eh-YAHZH?

Is this item on sale?
Cet article est-il en solde?
Set ahrt-EE-kl ess-TEEL on SOLD?

Do you have this in a smaller/larger size?
Avez-vous cela dans une taille plus petite/grande?
AH-veh VOO suh-LAH duhN oon TIE-yuh ploo peteet/GRONd?

Can I use this coupon on my purchase?
Puis-je utiliser ce coupon pour mon achat?
PWEEDZH ew-tee-lee-ZAY suh koo-POHN poor mohn AH-sha?

Can I pay with a credit card?
Puis-je payer avec une carte de crédit?
PWEEDZH pay-YAY ah-vek oon kahrt duh KRAY-dee?

Where do I go to check out?
Où dois-je aller pour payer?
OO dwahzh ahl-AY poor pay-YAY?

Do you offer gift wrapping?
Offrez-vous un service d'emballage-cadeau?
OH-freh VOO uhN sair-VEES dahm-blahzh kah-DOH?

How much is shipping to my address?
Combien coûte la livraison à mon adresse?
KOM-bee-yen KOOT lah leev-ray-ZHAWN ah mohn ah-DRESS?

When can I expect my order to arrive?
Quand puis-je m'attendre à recevoir ma commande?
KahN pweezh zhuh mohn-TAH-ndruh ah ruh-suh-VWAHR ma koh-MAWND?

Can I track my package?
Puis-je suivre mon colis?
PWEEDZH swee-vruh mohn koh-LEE?

Is there a fee for returns/exchanges?
Y a-t-il des frais pour les retours/échanges?
EEZ-tair day frah poor lay ruh-TUR/ZHEKSZHAWN?

Can I cancel my order?
Puis-je annuler ma commande?
PWEEDZH ahn-yuh-lay ma koh-MAWND?

Are there any promotions or discounts available?
Y a-t-il des promotions ou des réductions disponibles?
EEZ-tair day proh-moh-SYAWN oo day ray-dooK-see-YAWN diss-pohn-EE-bluh?

What sizes do you carry?
Quelles tailles avez-vous?
KELL TIE-yuh ah-veh

Can you help me find my size?
Pouvez-vous m'aider à trouver ma taille?
Poo-vay VOO meh-EE-deh ah truh-VEH may TIE-yuh?

Do you offer alterations or tailoring services?
Offrez-vous des services de retouches ou de tailleur?
Oh-freh VOO day sair-VEES duh ruh-TOOSH oo duh TAH-yur?

Can I have my items shipped to a different address?
Puis-je faire livrer mes articles à une adresse différente?
PWEEDZH fair leev-ray mayz ar-tikl ah oon ah-DRESS DEE-fay-RAWT?

Can you recommend something that would go well with this item?
Pouvez-vous me recommander quelque chose qui irait bien avec cet article?
Poo-vay VOO muh ruh-koh-mahn-DAY kelk shohz kee ee-ray byaN ah-vehk set ahrt-EE-kl?

Is there a limit on the number of items I can purchase?
Y a-t-il une limite sur le nombre d'articles que je peux acheter?
EEZ-teel yooN LEE-meet sooR luh NOM-bruh dar-tikl kuh zhuh puh eh-shuh-TAY?

Can I get a discount if I buy multiple items?
Puis-je avoir une réduction si j'achète plusieurs articles?
Pweezh zhuh ah-VWAHR ewn ray-dook-syawn see zhah-sheht pluh-zhoor ar-tikl?

Do you have any eco-friendly or sustainable clothing options?
Avez-vous des options de vêtements respectueux de l'environnement ou durables?
Ah-veh VOO dayz op-see-YAWN duh vet-mawn ruh-speck-teuh duh lahN-vee-roN-mawn oo dur-abl?

How do I care for this item?
Comment dois-je prendre soin de cet article?
Koh-mahN dwahzh prahn-dr suhN duh set ahrt-EE-kl?

Can I get a gift receipt with my purchase?
Puis-je avoir un reçu-cadeau avec mon achat?
Pweezh zhuh ah-VWAHR uh ruh-SEW-kah-DOH ah-vehk mohn ah-SHA?

Do you have a loyalty program or rewards system?
Avez-vous un programme de fidélité ou un système de récompenses?
Ah-veh VOO uhN proh-GRAM duh fee-day-lee-tay oo uhN sis-taym duh ray-kohm-PENS?

What forms of payment do you accept?
Quelles formes de paiement acceptez-vous?
Kell fohrm duh pay-mawn ahk-sehp-teh VOO?

Can I pay with cash?
Puis-je payer en espèces?
Pweezh zhuh pay-YAY ahN ess-PAYS?

Do you have a size chart I can look at?
Avez-vous un tableau des tailles que je peux consulter?
Ah-veh VOO uhN tah-bl-oh day TIE-yuh kuh zhuh puh kohn-sool-TAY?

What is the material of this item?
De quoi est fait cet article?
Duh kwah eh fay set ahrt-EE-kl?

Do you offer free shipping?
Offrez-vous la livraison gratuite?
Oh-freh VOO lah leev-ray-ZHAWN grah-too-IT?

Can I pick up my order in-store?
Puis-je récupérer ma commande en magasin?
Pweezh zhuh rew-koo-peh-ray ma koh-MAWND ahN mah-ga-ZAN?

Do you have a sale section or clearance items?
Avez-vous une section de soldes oudes articles en liquidation?
Ah-veh VOO ewn sek-see-YAWN duh sol-duh oo dayz ar-tikl ahN lee-kee-dah-see-YAWN?

Can I return or exchange an item?
Puis-je retourner ou échanger un article?
Pweezh zhuh ruh-toor-nay oo ay-shan-zhay uhN ahrt-EE-kl?

How long does shipping usually take?
Combien de temps prend généralement la livraison?
Kohm-byaN duh tahN prehN-zhuh-ray luh leev-ray-ZHAWN?

Do you have any promotions or special deals going on?
Avez-vous des promotions ou des offres spéciales en cours?
Ah-veh VOO day proh-moh-see-YAWN oo day zofr spay-see-YALL ahN koors?

Can I track my package once it's been shipped?
Puis-je suivre mon colis une fois qu'il a été expédié?
Pweezh zhuh swee-vruh mohn koh-LEEZ ewn fwa k-eel ah eh-tay eks-pay-dee-AY?

Is it possible to cancel my order?
Est-il possible d'annuler ma commande?
Ess-teel poh-see-bl dah-noo-lay ma koh-MAWND?

Do you have any recommendations for how to style this item?
Avez-vous des recommandations pour comment styler cet article?
Ah-veh VOO day ruh-koh-mahn-day-SYAWN poor koh-mahn STEE-lay set ahrt-EE-kl?

Can I try this item on before purchasing it?
Puis-je essayer cet article avant de l'acheter?
Pweezh zhuh ess-ah-yay set ahrt-EE-kl ah-vahN duh lah-shuh-tay?

Are there any additional fees or taxes I should be aware of?
Y a-t-il des frais ou taxes supplémentaires dont je devrais être consciente?
Ee ah-TEEL day fray oo tahks soo-play-mahN-tehr doN zhuh duh-vrayz eht-tre cohN-see-ahnt?

Do you offer alterations or tailoring services?
Offrez-vous des services de retouches ou de couture?
Oh-freh VOO day ser-veess duh ruh-toosh oo duh koo-tuhr?

Is there a warranty or guarantee for this item?
Y a-t-il une garantie pour cet article?
Ee ah-TEEL ewn gah-rahn-TEE poor set ahrt-EE-kl?

Can I place an order over the phone or online only?
Puis-je passer une commande par téléphone ou uniquement en ligne?
*Pweezh zhuh pah-say ewn koh-mahNd pahr teh-lay-FOHN oo
o-nee-kee-mahN ahN leen?*

SIMPLE QUESTIONS AND ANSWERS

What's your name?
Comment vous appelez-vous ?
KOH-MOHN vooz AP-uh-lay VOO?

My name is [insert name here].
Je m'appelle [insert name here].
ZHuh ma-PELL [insert name here].

How old are you?
Quel âge avez-vous ?
KEHL AHZH AV-ay VOO?

I'm [insert age here] years old.
J'ai [insert age here] ans.
ZHAY [insert age here] AHNS.

Where are you from?
D'où venez-vous ?
DOO VUH-NAY VOO?

I'm from [insert country or city here].
Je viens de [insert country or city here].
ZHuh VYAN duh [insert country or city here].

What do you do?
Que faites-vous dans la vie ?
Kuh FET-uh VOO dahn lah VEE?

I'm a [insert profession or job title here].
Je suis [insert profession or job title here].
ZHuh SWEE [insert profession or job title here].

What's your favorite color?
Quelle est votre couleur préférée ?
KELL AY VOT-ruh koo-LUHR PRAY-FAY-RAY?

My favorite color is [insert color here].
Ma couleur préférée est [insert color here].
Mah koo-LUHR PRAY-FAY-RAY ay [insert color here].

What's your favorite food?
Quel est votre plat préféré ?
KELL AY VOT-ruh plah PRAY-FAY-RAY?

My favorite food is [insert food here].
Mon plat préféré est [insert food here].
Moh plah PRAY-FAY-RAY ay [insert food here].

What's your favorite movie?
Quel est votre film préféré ?
KELL AY VOT-ruh feelm PRAY-FAY-RAY?

My favorite movie is [insert movie title here].
Mon film préféré est [insert movie title here].
Moh feelm PRAY-FAY-RAY ay [insert movie title here].

What's your favorite book?
Quel est votre livre préféré ?
KELL AY VOT-ruh LEEV PRAY-FAY-RAY?

My favorite book is [insert book title here].
Mon livre préféré est [insert book title here].
Moh LEEV PRAY-FAY-RAY ay [insert book title here].

What's your favorite hobby?
Quel est votre passe-temps préféré ?
KELL AY VOT-ruh PAHS-uh-TAHM PRAY-FAY-RAY?

My favorite hobby is [insert hobby here].
Mon passe-temps préféré est [insert hobby here].
Moh PAHS-uh-TAHM PRAY-FAY-RAY ay [insert hobby here].

Are you married?
Êtes-vous mariée ?
ET-VUH mah-ree-AYE?

No, I'm not married.
Non, je ne suis pas mariée.
NOHN, zhuh nuh SWEE pah mah-ree-AYE.

Do you have any siblings?
Avez-vous des frères et sœurs ?
AH-veh-VOO day FRAY-ruh ZAY SUHR?

Yes, I have [insert number of siblings here] siblings.
Oui, j'ai [insert number of siblings here] frères et sœurs.
WEE, zhay [insert number of siblings here] FRAY-ruh ZAY SUHR.

What's your favorite animal?
Quel est votre animal préféré ?
KELL AY VOT-ruh an-nee-MAHL PRAY-FAY-RAY?

My favorite animal is [insert animal here].
Mon animal préféré est [insert animal here].
Moh-n an-nee-MAHL PRAY-FAY-RAY ay [insert animal here].

What's your favorite season?
Quelle est votre saison préférée ?
KELL AY VOT-ruh SAH-zawn PRAY-FAY-RAY?

My favorite season is [insert season here].
Ma saison préférée est [insert season here].
Mah SAH-zawn PRAY-FAY-RAY ay [insert season here].

Do you have any pets?
Avez-vous des animaux domestiques ?
AH-veh-VOO dayz an-nee-MOH doh-MES-teeK?

Yes, I have [insert number of pets here] pets.
Oui, j'ai [insert number of pets here] animaux domestiques.
WEE, zhay [insert number of pets here] an-nee-MOH doh-MES-teeK

ASKING FOR AND GIVING DIRECTIONS

*Insert the location where applicable.

Excuse me, could you tell me how to get to ___?
Excusez-moi, pouvez-vous me dire comment aller à ___?
Ehk-SKUU-zay mwah, puuh-VEY-voo muh DEER kuh-MON ah ___ ?

I'm lost, can you help me find my way?
Je suis perdue, pouvez-vous m'aider à retrouver mon chemin?
Juh swee pair-DUH, puuh-VEY-voo meh-DAY ah retruh-VAY mohn shuh-MANG?

Could you give me directions to ___?
Pourriez-vous m'indiquer le chemin pour aller à ___?
POO-ree-vey voo mahn-dee-KEY luh shuh-MANG poor ah-LEY ah ___ ?

Which way should I go to get to ___?
Dans quelle direction dois-je aller pour arriver à ___?
Dahn kell dir-EK-shon dwahzh AL-ley poor ah-REE-vay ah ___ ?

Is there a ___ nearby?
Est-ce qu'il y a une ___ à proximité?
Ess-kuh eel yah uh uhn ___ ah proh-KSEE-mee-TAY?

How far is it to ___?
C'est loin de ___?
Say lwahn duh ___ ?

Could you point me in the right direction?
Pourriez-vous m'orienter dansla bonne direction?
POO-ree-vey voo more-ee-awn-tay dahn lah BOHN dir-EK-shon?

Excuse me, is this the way to ___?
Excusez-moi, est-ce que c'est par ici pour aller à ___?
Ehk-SKUU-zay mwah, ess-kuh say pahr ee-see poor ah-LEY ah ___ ?

I'm trying to find ___ street. Do you know where it is?
Je cherche la rue ___ . Savez-vous où elle se trouve?
Juh shairsh lah roo ___. sav-ey voo oo ell suh troov?

Can you show me on a map how to get to ___?
Pourriez-vous me montrer sur une carte comment aller à ___?
POO-ree-vey voo muh mohn-TREH sewr ewn kart kuh-MON ah ___?

Go straight ahead.
Allez tout droit.
Ah-LAY too drwah

Turn left/right.
Tournez à gauche/à droite.
Toor-NEY ah GOSH/ah DWAT

Take the first/second/third street on your left/right.
Prenez la première/deuxième/troisième rue à gauche/à droite.
Pruh-NAY lah PREH-myer/duh-zee-EM/twah-zee-EM rwe ah GOSH/ah DWAT

Cross the bridge/intersection.
Traversez le pont/le carrefour.
Trah-ver-SAY luh pohn/luh kahr-fuhr

Continue until you see ___ on your left/right.
Continuez jusqu'à ce que vous voyiez ___ sur votre gauche/droite.
Kon-teen-OO zhoo-SKAH seuh kuh voo vwah-YAY ___ sur vohtre goosh/dwat

It's just around the corner.
C'est juste après le coin de la rue.
Say joo-stuh ah-PREH luh kwahn duh lah roo

You'll see ___ on your left/right.
Vous verrez ___ sur votre gauche/droite.
Voo veh-RAY ___ sur vohtre goosh/dwat

It's on your left/right.
C'est sur votre gauche/droite.
Say sur vohtre goosh/dwat

It's across from ___ .
C'est en face de ___ .
Say ahn fahs duh ___

Go straight ahead.
Allez tout droit.
AH-leh too drwah.

Turn left/right at the intersection.
Tournez à gauche/droite à l'intersection.
TOOR-neh ah gohsh/dwah a lahn-tehr-sehk-see-YOHn.

Take the first/second/third street on the left/right.
Prenez la première/deuxième/troisième rue à gauche/droite.
PREH-neh lah preh-MYEHR/duh-zee-EHM/trwah-ZYEHM rweh ah gohsh/dwaht.

It's on your left/right.
C'est à gauche/droite.
SEH tah gohsh/dwaht.

You'll see a big building on your left/right.
Vous verrez un grand bâtiment à gauche/droite.
VOO veh-reh uhn grahn bah-TEE-mehn ah gohsh/dwaht.

Keep walking until you reach the roundabout.
Continuez à marcher jusqu'au rond-point.
KON-ti-nu-ehz ah mar-SHEY zhoo-kuh rohn-PWAN.

Cross the street at the traffic lights.
Traversez la rue au feu.
TRAH-ver-seh lah rew oh FUH.

Walk down the alley until you reach the end.
Descendez l'allée jusqu'au bout.
Deh-SEHN-deh lah-LAY zhoo-koo BOO.

Turn back and walk towards the park.
Retournez-vous et marchez vers le parc.
Ruh-TOUR-neh VOO eh mar-SHEY vehr luh PARC.

Go through the tunnel.
Passez par le tunnel.
Pah-SEH par luh toon-EL.

Take the stairs up/down.
Prenez les escaliers en haut/en bas.
PREH-neh leh-zeh-skah-LYEHZ ahn oh/ahn bah.

Walk past the supermarket on your left.
Passez devant le supermarché sur votre gauche.
Pah-SEH dev-AHn luh soo-pehr-mar-SHEY sur voh-truh gohsh.

Go under the bridge.
Passez sous le pont.
Pah-SEH soo luh pohn.

It's just around the corner.
C'est juste au coin.
SEH zhoost oh KWAH.

You can't miss it.
Vous ne pouvez pas le rater.
Voo nuh poovay pah luh RAH-teh

Can you give me directions to _____?
Pouvez-vous me donner des indications pour aller à _____ ?
Poo-VEH-VOO muh DOH-neh day zan-dee-kah-see-ohn pour ah-LAY ah _____ ?

Excuse me, do you know how to get to _____?
Excusez-moi, savez-vous comment aller à _____ ?
EX-kew-ZAY-MWAH, sah-VEH-VOO koh-mahn ah-LAY ah _____ ?

Could you tell me which way to go to get to _____?
Pourriez-vous me dire quel chemin prendre pour aller à _____ ?
POO-ree-eh-VOO muh DEER kell shuh-MEHN prahn-druh pour ah-LAY
ah _____ ?

I'm lost. Can you help me find my way to _____?
Je suis perdue. Pouvez-vous m'aider à trouver mon chemin pour aller à _____ ?
ZHUH SWEE pair-DUH. Poo-VEH-VOO meh-DEE ay-DAY ah truh-VEH
mohn shuh-MEHN pour ah-LAY ah _____ ?

I'm trying to get to _____, but I don't know how to get there.
J'essaie d'aller à _____, mais je ne sais pas comment y aller.
JEH-say dah-LAY ah _____, may zhuh nuh say pah koh-mahn ee
ah-LAY.

Sorry to bother you, but could you direct me to _____?
Désolée de vous déranger, pourriez-vous me diriger vers _____ ?
DAY-zoh-LAY duh VOO day-rahn-ZHAY, POO-ree-eh-VOO muh
DEE-ree-geh vair _____ ?

Can you point me in the direction of _____?
Pouvez-vous me montrer la direction de _____ ?
POO-veh-VOO muh mohn-TREH lah DEE-rek-see-ohn duh _____ ?

I need to find _____, do you know where it is?
J'ai besoin de trouver _____, savez-vous où c'est ?
ZHAY buh-ZWAHN duh troo-VAY _____, sah-VEH-VOO oo say ?

I'm looking for _____, could you give me directions?
Je cherche _____, pourriez-vous me donner des indications ?
ZHUH shairsh _____, POO-ree-eh-VOO muh DOH-neh day
zan-dee-kah-see-ohn ?

Do you happen to know how to get to _____ from here?
Savez-vous par hasard comment aller à _____ à partir d'ici ?
SAH-veh-VOO par ah-ZAHR koh-mahn ah-LAY ah _____ ah PAHR-teer
dee-SEE ?

Can you show me the way to _____?
Pouvez-vous me montrer le chemin pour aller à _____ ?
POO-veh-VOO muh mohn-TREH luh shuh-MEHN pour ah-LAY ah _____

I'm not familiar with this area, can you guide me to _____?
Je ne connais pas bien cette zone, pourriez-vous me guider jusqu'à _____ ?
ZHUH nuh koh-NAY pah bee-EN set ZOHN, POO-ree-eh-VOO muh GHEE-day jusk ah

I'm not familiar with this area, can you guide me to _____?
Je ne connais pas bien la région, pouvez-vous me guider vers _____ ?
ZHuh nuh kohn-NAY pah byan lah ray-jyohn, puh-veh-VOO muh ghee-day vair _____ ?

I'm trying to find my way to _____, can you help me?
Je cherche mon chemin pour aller à _____, pouvez-vous m'aider ?
ZHUH shairsh mohn shuh-MEHN pour ah-LAY ah _____, puh-veh-VOO meh-DAY ?

I'm having trouble finding _____, can you tell me how to get there?
Je rencontre des difficultés à trouver _____, pouvez-vous m'indiquer comment y arriver ?
ZHuh ruhn-kohn-truh day dee-fee-kee-TAY ah troo-VAY _____, puh-veh-VOO man-DEE-kay koh-mahn ee ah-ree-VAY ?

Excuse me, could you direct me to the nearest _____?
Excusez-moi, pouvez-vous m'indiquer le chemin pour aller au _____ le plus proche ?
EX-kew-zay-MWAH, puh-veh-VOO man-DEE-kay luh shuh-MEHN pour ah-LAY oh _____ luh ploo prosh ?

Can you tell me which way I should go to get to _____?
Pouvez-vous me dire quel chemin prendre pour aller à _____ ?
Poo-veh-VOO muh DEER kell shuh-MEHN prahn-druh pour ah-LAY ah _____ ?

I'm trying to get to _____, but I'm not sure which direction to go.
Je cherche à aller à _____, mais je ne suis pas sûre de la direction à prendre.
ZHUH shairsh ah ah-LAY ah _____, may zhuh nuh swee pah SYUR duh lah dee-rek-see-ohn ah prahn-druh.

Could you please give me directions to _____?
Pourriez-vous s'il vous plaît m'indiquer comment aller à _____ ?
POO-ree-eh-VOO SEEL-VOO-PLAY man-DEE-kay koh-mahn ah-LAY ah _____ ?

I'm new in town and I need to find _____, could you help me out?
Je suis nouveau / nouvelle en ville et j'ai besoin de trouver _____, pouvez-vous m'aider ?
ZHuh swee noo-VOH / noo-VELL ahn veel ay zhay buh-ZWAHN duh troo-VAY _____, puh-veh-VOO meh-DAY ?

I'm trying to find my way around here, could you give me some directions?
J'essaie de me repérer ici, pourriez-vous me donner quelques indications ?
Juh-SAY duh muh ruh-PEAR-ay ee-SEE, POO-ree-eh-VOO muh DOH-neh kelk zan-dee-kah-see-ohn ?

I'm looking for the best way to get to _____, can you assist me?
Je cherche le meilleur moyen d'aller à _____, pouvez-vous m'aider ?
Je SHERSH le mey-YEUR mey-YEN d'ahl-AY a _____, POU-vey-voo meh-DAY ?

Could you please show me how to get to _____?
Pouvez-vous me montrer comment aller à _____, s'il vous plaît ?
Pou-vey-voo muh mohn-TREH koh-mahn tah-LAY a _____, SEEL voo-PLAY ?

I'm trying to find my way back to my hotel, can you tell me which way to go?
J'essaie de retrouver mon chemin vers mon hôtel, pouvez-vous me dire quelle direction prendre ?
Jeh-SAY d'ess-AY deuh ruh-troo-VAY mon sha-MEN vehr mohn oh-TEL, pou-vey-voo muh DEER kell di-REK-see-ON prahn-druh ?

Can you direct me to the nearest gas station?

Pouvez-vous me diriger vers la station-service la plus proche ?

Pou-vey-voo muh deer-ee-GAY vehr la sta-see-on-ser-VEES la ploo prosh ?

I need to get to _____ as soon as possible, could you give me directions?

J'ai besoin d'aller à _____ dès que possible, pourriez-vous me donner les indications ?

J'ai beh-SWAHN d'ahl-AY a _____ dehs kuh pos-SEE-bl, puhr-VEY-voo muh don-NAY ley zihn-dee-kah-SEE-ON ?

Can you tell me how to get to _____ from here?

Pouvez-vous me dire comment aller à _____ à partir d'ici ?

Pou-vey-voo muh deer koh-mahn tah-LAY a _____ ah par-TEER dee-SEE

Sorry, I'm a little lost, could you help me find my way to _____?

Excusez-moi, je suis un peu perdue, pourriez-vous m'aider à trouver le chemin de _____ ?

Ex-KUZ-ay mwah, je swee uhn peu per-DUH, puhr-vey-voo meh-DAY truh-VAY ley she-MEHN duh _____ ?

Can you please give me clear directions to _____?

Pourriez-vous s'il vous plaît me donner des directions claires pour aller à _____ ?

Pou-vey-voo seel voo-PLAY meh-don-NAY de-rek-see-ON klaire poor al-AY a _____ ?

COMMON BUSINESS STATEMENTS AND QUESTIONS

Can I help you with anything?
Puis-je vous aider en quoi que ce soit ?
PWEESH-JUH voo zeh-DEH ay-DEH on kwah suh SWAH?

Thank you for your business.
Merci pour votre entreprise.
MEHR-SEE poor voh-TRUH ahn-tre-PRENN

Please let me know if you have any questions.
S'il vous plaît, faites-moi savoir si vous avez des questions.
SEEL VOUS PLAIT, fet-MWAH sah-VOIR si voo zah-VAY day KES-tee-yons.

What are your business hours?
Quels sont vos horaires d'ouverture ?
KELL sohn vohr-OR doo-VER-TOOR?

We have a wide variety of products/services.
Nous avons une grande variété de produits/services.
NOOZ ah-VOHNZ oon GRAND vah-ree-AY-tay duh proh-DEE/SER-vees.

How may I assist you?
Comment puis-je vous aider ?
KOH-mohn PWEESH-JUH voo zeh-DEH?

What's the purpose of your visit?
Quel est l'objet de votre visite ?
KELL eh loh-BJAY duh voh-TRUH vee-ZEET?

We have a special promotion going on.
Nous avons une promotion spéciale en cours.
NOOZ ah-VOHNZ oon proh-moh-see-YON spay-see-AHL ahn KOOR.

Would you like to schedule a meeting?
Souhaitez-vous planifier une réunion ?
SOO-eh-teh VOO pleh-nee-FYAY oon ruh-YOHN?

Our company is committed to quality.
Notre entreprise est engagée envers la qualité.
NO-truh ahn-tre-PRENN eh ahn-ga-JAY on-vair la kah-lee-TAY.

Could you please clarify your request?
Pourriez-vous préciser votre demande, s'il vous plaît ?
POOR-REE-YEH VOO prey-SEE-ZAY vo-truh duh-MAHND, SEEL VOO PLAIT?

Can you provide me with more details?
Pourriez-vous me fournir plus de détails, s'il vous plaît ?
POOR-REE-YEH VOO muh foor-NEER ploo duh DAY-tay, SEEL VOO PLAIT?

What is your budget for this project?
Quel est votre budget pour ce projet ?
KELL eh vo-truh booj-JAY poor suh proh-JAY?

I'm sorry, but that's not possible.
Je suis désolée, mais ce n'est pas possible.
ZHuh swee day-zo-LAY, may suh ney pah possible.

We offer a satisfaction guarantee.
Nous offrons une garantie de satisfaction.
NOOZ oh-FRONZ oon gar-an-TEE duh sah-tees-fahk-see-YON.

Is there anything else you need?
Avez-vous besoin de quelque chose d'autre
AH-vey VOO b'swahn duh kel-kuh shohz d'OTRUH?

How can I help you be more productive?
Comment puis-je vous aider à être plus productif ?
Koh-mohn PWEESH-JUH voo zeh-DEH ah eh-truh ploo proh-duhk-TEEF?

Our prices are competitive.
Nos prix sont compétitifs.
NO pree sohn kohn-pet-ee-TEEF.

Please fill out this form.
Veuillez remplir ce formulaire, s'il vous plaît.
VUH-yay rahn-PLEER suh for-mew-LAIR, SEEL VOO PLAIT.

What's your preferred method of payment?
Quelle est votre méthode de paiement préférée ?
KELL eh vo-truh may-thod duh PAY-mohn prey-FAY-RAY?

We provide excellent customer service.
Nous offrons un excellent service à la clientèle.
NOOZ oh-FRONZ uhn ehks-ELL-ahn ser-VEES ah la klee-YAN-tell.

Can I have your contact information?
Puis-je avoir vos coordonnées, s'il vous plaît ?
POO-ee-JUH ah-VWAHR vo koh-or-doh-NAY, SEEL VOO PLAIT?

What are your company's values?
Quelles sont les valeurs de votre entreprise ?
KELL sohn ley vah-LEUR duh vo-truh ahn-TRE-prize?

Our team is highly skilled and experienced.
Notre équipe est hautement qualifiée et expérimentée.
NO-truh eh-KEEP eh o-TUH-men kah-lee-FEE-eh eh eks-peer-ee-men-TAY.

How soon do you need this completed?
À quelle date avez-vous besoin que cela soit terminé ?
AH kell DAT ah-vey VOO b'swahn kuh suh-LAH swa term-in-AY?

Do you have any feedback or suggestions?
Avez-vous des commentaires ou des suggestions ?
AH-vey VOO day koh-mahn-TAIR oo day soo-jes-tee-OHN?

We are committed to sustainability.
Nous sommes engagés envers la durabilité.
NOOZ som zon-gah-ZAY on-vair la dew-rah-bee-LI-TAY.

How can we improve our service?
Comment pouvons-nous améliorer notre service ?
Koh-mohn poo-vohn-NOO ah-mey-lee-or-AY no-truh ser-VEES?

Can we set up a follow-up call/meeting?
Pouvons-nous organiser un appel/réunion de suivi ?
Poo-vohn-NOO zor-gah-nee-ZAY uhn ah-PAY/RAY-yun-yon duh swi-vee?

Let's start with the initial proposal.

Commençons par la proposition initiale.

Koh-mah-SON pahr lah proh-poh-ZEE-syon een-ee-see-YAHL.

We need to identify our common interests.

Nous devons identifier nos intérêts communs.

NOO duh-VOH idehn-tee-FYEH nohz AN-teh-reh KOM-muhN.

Can we find a middle ground that works for both parties?

Pouvons-nous trouver un terrain d'entente qui convient aux deux parties ?

POO-vohn noo troo-VAY uhN tay-rahn-dahNt kee kohn-VYEH oh day PARR-tee?

Let's discuss the timeline for implementation.

Discutons du calendrier de mise en œuvre.

DEE-skoo-TOHNG dew kah-lahn-dree deh meez ahn EUV-ruh.

We need to consider the budget constraints.

Nous devons tenir compte des contraintes budgétaires.

NOO duh-VOH tahn-DEE kohNt day kon-traint BOO-jeh-tair.

Can we negotiate on the payment terms?

Pouvons-nous négocier les modalités de paiement ?

POO-vohn noo neh-goh-see-eh lay moh-dah-lee-TAY duh pay-mahn?

Let's discuss the scope of the project.

Discutons de l'envergure du projet.

DEE-skoo-TOHNG duh lahn-vair-GYUR duh proh-JAY.

We need to clarify the roles and responsibilities of each party.

Nous devons clarifier les rôles et responsabilités de chaque partie.

NOO duh-VOH klah-ree-FYEH lay rohl ay ray-spohn-sah-bee-lih-TAY duh shak PARR-tee.

Can we discuss the potential risks and challenges?
Pouvons-nous discuter des risques et des défis potentiels ?
*POO-vohn noo dee-skoo-TEH day REESK ay day day-fee
poh-tahn-sy-EL?*

Let's explore options for mutual benefit.
Explorons les options pour un bénéfice mutuel.
Ex-plor-ohn layz op-see-YOHN poor uh bay-nuh-fees myoo-TWEL.

We need to review and finalize the contract.
Nous devons revoir et finaliser le contrat.
NOO duh-VOH ruh-vwahr ay fee-na-lee-ZAY luh kon-trah.

Can we agree on the terms and conditions?
Pouvons-nous nous entendre sur les termes et conditions ?
POO-vohn noo nooz ahN-tahNDR sur lay term ay kohn-dih-syon.

We need to negotiate a win-win situation.
Nous devons négocier une situation gagnant-gagnant.
*NOO duh-vohn nuh-goh-see-ay oo-nuh sit-yoo-ah-see-ohn
GAH-nyahn-GAH-nyahn.*

Can we discuss the deliverables and deadlines?
Pouvons-nous discuter des livrables et des délais ?
POO-vohn noo dee-skoo-tay day liv-ruh-bluh ay day day-lay.

Let's brainstorm ideas and solutions.
Laissons-nous réfléchir aux idées et aux solutions.
LEH-sohn noo ray-flay-sheer oh zee-day ay oh soo-lee-see-ohn.

We need to come up with a feasible plan.
Nous devons élaborer un plan réalisable.
NOO duh-vohn ay-lah-bor-ay uh plahn ray-ah-lee-zah-bluh.

Can we consider alternative options?
Pouvons-nous envisager des options alternatives ?
POO-vohn noo ahn-vee-zah-zhay dayz ohp-see-ohnz al-tair-nah-teev.

Let's analyze the market trends and competition.

Analysons les tendances du marché et la concurrence.

AH-nah-lee-sohn lay tan-dahns dy mar-shay ay lah kohn-koo-rahns.

We need to reach a compromise that satisfies both parties.

Nous devons parvenir à un compromis qui satisfait les deux parties.

NOO duh-vohn pahr-ve-nir ah uh kohn-proh-mee kee sah-tee-fay leh DUH pahr-tee.

Can we negotiate the terms of the contract?

Pouvons-nous négocier les termes du contrat ?

POO-vohn noo neh-goh-see-ay lay tairm dyu kon-trah.

Let's review the key points of the agreement.

Examinons les points clés de l'accord.

EHg-zah-mahn-yohn ley PWAH deh lah-kohr.

We need to make sure that the deal is mutually beneficial.

Nous devons nous assurer que l'accord est mutuellement bénéfique.

NOO duh-VOH noo-zah-SUR kuh lah-kohr eh mew-tew-ehl-mawn bay-nay-fee-kee.

Can we discuss the terms of payment in detail?

Pouvons-nous discuter des modalités de paiement en détail?

POO-vohn noo DEES-koo-tey deh moh-dah-lee-tey duh pay-uh-mawn ahn deh-TAY?

We need to find a solution that meets everyone's needs.

Nous devons trouver une solution qui répond aux besoins de chacun.

NOO duh-VOH truh-VEY ewn soh-lu-see-yohn kee rah-POHN oh neh-swa deh shah-kawn.

Can we discuss the pricing and costs involved?

Pouvons-nous discuter des tarifs et des coûts impliqués?

POO-vohn noo DEES-koo-tey deh tah-reef ey deh kooz ahm-plee-KEY?

STAYING AT A HOTEL

I would like to book a room for two nights, please.
Je voudrais réserver une chambre pour deux nuits, s'il vous plaît.
ZHuh voo-DREH ruh-zehr-VAY oon shahmbr pohr DUH nwee, SEEL VOUS PLAIT?

What is the price of your cheapest room?
Quel est le prix de votre chambre la moins chère ?
KELL EH luh pree duh voh-truh shahmbr la MWAN share?

Do you have any rooms available for tonight?
Avez-vous des chambres disponibles pour ce soir ?
AH-veh VOO day shahmbr deez-PONI-bluh poor suh SWAHR?

Can I get a discount if I book for a longer period?
Est-ce que je peux avoir une réduction si je réserve pour une période plus longue ?
ESS-kuh zhuh PUH ah-VOO-ar oon ruh-DUK-see-YON si zhuh ruh-ZAIRV poor oon pair-EE-ud plew lawng?

Is breakfast included in the room rate?
Est-ce que le petit-déjeuner est inclus dans le prix de la chambre ?
ESS-kuh luh puh-tee day-JUH-nay EH in-CLUE dahn luh pree duh la shahmbr?

What time is check-in/check-out?
À quelle heure est l'heure d'arrivée/de départ ?
AH KELL UHR EH luh-HEUR dah-REE-VAY/duh DEH-pahr?

Do you have a shuttle service to the airport/train station?
Avez-vous un service de navette pour l'aéroport/la gare ?
AH-veh VOO uhn SAIR-vees duh nah-VET poor lah-EH-roh-POR/la gahr?

Can I book a room with a view?
Est-ce que je peux réserver une chambre avec vue ?
ESS-kuh zhuh PUH ruh-ZAIR-vay oon shahmbr ah-VEK VUE?

Are pets allowed in the hotel?
Les animaux de compagnie sont-ils autorisés dans l'hôtel ?
LAY anee-MO deh kawn-pahn-YEH sohn-TEEL aw-toh-ree-ZAY dahn loh-TEL?

Is there a gym/pool in the hotel?
Y a-t-il une salle de sport / une piscine dans l'hôtel ?
EE ah-TEEL oon SAHL duh spohr / oon pee-SEEN dahn loh-TEL?

Do you have a restaurant on site?
Avez-vous un restaurant sur place ?
AH-veh VOO uhn reh-stoh-RAHN sur plahs?

How far is the hotel from the city center?
À quelle distance se trouve l'hôtel du centre-ville ?
AH KELL dees-TAHNS suh troov l'ho-TEL duh sahntruh-VEEL?

Can I pay with cash or credit card?
Est-ce que je peux payer en espèces ou par carte de crédit ?
ESS-kuh zhuh PUH pay-YAY ahn es-PES oh pahr KART duh kray-DEE?

Is there a deposit required when booking a room?
Est-ce qu'un dépôt est requis lors de la réservation d'une chambre ?
ESS-kuh uhn day-POH EH ruh-KEEZ lohr duh la ray-zair-VAH-syohn d'oon sh

Is there a deposit required when booking a room?
Est-ce qu'un dépôt est requis lors de la réservation d'une chambre ?
ESS-kuh uhn day-POH EH ruh-KEEZ lohr duh la ray-zair-VAH-syohn d'oon shahmbr?

Do you offer room service?
Offrez-vous un service en chambre ?
OH-freh-VOO uhn sair-VEES ahn shahmbr?

Can I request a late check-out?
Est-ce que je peux demander un départ tardif ?
ESS-kuh zhuh PUH deh-MAN-day uhn DEH-pahr tar-DEEF?

Is there a minibar in the room?
Y a-t-il un minibar dans la chambre ?
EE ah-TEEL uhn mee-nee-BAR dahn la shahmbr?

Are there smoking and non-smoking rooms available?
Y a-t-il des chambres fumeur et non-fumeur disponibles ?
EE ah-TEEL day shahmbr fuh-MUHR ay nohn-fuh-MUHR dees-PONI-bluh?

Is there free Wi-Fi in the hotel?
Est-ce qu'il y a du Wi-Fi gratuit dans l'hôtel ?
ESS-kuh eel EE ah doo Wi-Fi groo-ee-TAHN dahn loh-TEL?

Can I cancel my booking and get a refund?
Est-ce que je peux annuler ma réservation et obtenir un remboursement ?
ESS-kuh zhuh PUH ah-noo-LAY mah ray-zair-vah-SYON ay ohb-teh-NEER uhn ra-mboor-suh-mawn?

What is your cancellation policy?
Quelle est votre politique d'annulation ?
KELL EH voh-truh po-lee-TEEK dah-noo-la-see-YON?

Is there a safe in the room?
Y a-t-il un coffre-fort dans la chambre ?
EE ah-TEEL uhn koffr-FOHR dahn la shahmbr?

How often are the rooms cleaned?
À quelle fréquence les chambres sont-elles nettoyées ?
AH kell fre-konss lay shahmbr sohn-tell neht-wah-YAY?

Can I request extra towels/bedding?
Est-ce que je peux demander des serviettes/literies supplémentaires ?
ESS-kuh zhuh PUH duh-man-DAY day sehr-VYET/li-tuh-REE soo-pleh-MON-teh-air?

Is there a parking facility available?
Y a-t-il une facilité de stationnement disponible ?
EE ah-TEEL ewn fah-si-lee-TAY duh stah-syon-MAWN dee-poh-NEE-bluh?

Is the hotel accessible for people with disabilities?
L'hôtel est-il accessible aux personnes handicapées ?
LOH-tel ess-TEEL ahk-seh-SEE-bluh oh puh-rSONN ahn-dee-KA-peh?

Do you have a loyalty program?
Avez-vous un programme de fidélité ?
Ah-veh-VOO uh proh-GRAHM duh fee-deh-lee-TAY?

Can I book a room for a special occasion?
Est-ce que je peux réserver une chambre pour une occasion spéciale ?
ESS-kuh zhuh PUH ruh-zair-VAY ewn shahmbr poor ewn
ok-kah-zee-YON speh-see-AL?

Is there a concierge service available?
Y a-t-il un service de conciergerie disponible ?
EE ah-TEEL uhn sair-VEES duh kon-see-air-zhuh-REE dEE-poh-NEE-bluh?

Do you offer any tours or activities for guests?
Offrez-vous des visites ou des activités pour les invités ?
OH-freh-VOO day vee-ZEET oo day-z-ak-tee-VEE-tay poor layz
ahn-vee-TAY?

What's the weather like today?
Quel temps fait-il aujourd'hui?
KELL tahn fay-TEEL oh-zhur-DWEE?

Is it supposed to rain/snow later?
Est-ce qu'il est prévu de la pluie/de la neige plus tard ?
EHSS-kuh EEL eh prey-VOO duh lah plew/duh lah nehzhe ploo tar?

What's the temperature right now?
Quelle est la température actuelle?
KELL eh lah tomp-ehr-ahtoor ahk-TELL?

Is it hot outside?
Est-ce qu'il fait chaud dehors?
EHSS-kuh EEL fay SHOW duh-OR?

Is it cold outside?
Est-ce qu'il fait froid dehors?
EHSS-kuh EEL fay frawd duh-OR?

What's the temperature?
Quelle est la température?
KELL eh lah tomp-ehr-ahtoor?

Will it be sunny tomorrow?
Est-ce qu'il fera beau demain?
EHSS-kuh EEL fuh-RAH boh duh-MANG?

Is there a chance of thunderstorms?
Y a-t-il des risques d'orages?
EE ah-TEEL day reesk dor-AJH?

Is it going to snow?
Est-ce qu'il va neiger?
EHSS-kuh EEL vah NEHZH-ee?

What's the forecast for tomorrow?
Quelle est la prévision pour demain?
KELL eh lah pray-vee-ZYOHNG poor duh-MANG?

Is it windy outside?
Est-ce qu'il y a du vent dehors?
EHSS-kuh EEL ee ah doo vahn duh-OR?

What's the humidity like?
Quel est le taux d'humidité?
KELL eh luh toh doo-meedee-TAY?

Is it foggy outside?
Est-ce qu'il y a du brouillard dehors?
EHSS-kuh EEL ee ah doo broo-yahr duh-OR?

Will it be clear tonight?
Est-ce que le ciel sera dégagé ce soir?
EHSS-kuh luh see-EL seh-RAH day-gah-JAY suh SWAHR?

Is it going to be humid?
Est-ce que l'air sera humide?
EHSS-kuh lair seh-RAH yoo-MEED?

What's the chance of precipitation?
Quel est le risque de précipitations?
KELL eh luh reesk duh pray-see-peeta-see-YOHNG?

How hot does it get here in the summer?
Quelle est la température maximale en été ici ?
KELL eh lah tomp-ehr-ahtoor mak-SEE-mahl on eh-TAY ee-see?

How cold does it get here in the winter?
À quelle température descend-il ici en hiver ?
AH kell tomp-ehr-ahtoor day-sahn-DEEL ee-see on ee-VAYR?

Is there a hurricane coming?
Est-ce qu'un ouragan arrive ?
EHSS-kuh un oo-RAH-gahn ah-REEV?

What's the UV index?
Quel est l'indice UV ?
KELL eh lahN-deese YOO-veh?

Are there any weather warnings?
Y a-t-il des alertes météo ?
EE ah-TEEL dayz ah-LEHRT may-tay-oh?

Have areas been affected by flooding?
Est-ce que des zones ont été touchées par des inondations ?
EHSS-kuh day ZOHNZ ohn-teh TOO-shay par dayz
een-ohn-dah-see-YOHNG?

Is it safe to travel in this weather?
Est-ce que c'est sûr de voyager par ce temps ?
EHSS-kuh seh SOOR duh vwah-YAH-zhay par suh tahN?

Will the weather affect my flight?
Est-ce que le temps affectera mon vol ?
EHSS-kuh luh tahN ah-fek-TEH-rah mohN vol?

Do you know what the forecast is for tomorrow?
Savez-vous quelle est la prévision pour demain ?
SAH-veh voo kell eh lah pray-vee-ZYOHNG poor duh-MANG?

Are there any weather warnings or alerts in effect?
Y a-t-il des avertissements ou des alertes météo en vigueur ?
EE ah-TEEL dayz ah-ver-tees-mahn oo dayz ah-lehrt may-tay-oh ahN
vee-guhr?

It's a beautiful day outside.
Il fait beau dehors.
EEL feh BOH duh-OR.

I love when it rains - it's so relaxing.
J'aime quand il pleut - c'est tellement relaxant.
JEM kahn EEL pluh - seh tehl-MANG ruh-lahk-SAHNG.

WORKING OUT AT A GYM

What are the gym hours?
Quelles sont les heures d'ouverture de la salle de sport ?
KELL sohn lay UR dou-vair-ture duh sahl duh spohr?

Do you have any classes today?
Avez-vous des cours aujourd'hui ?
Ah-VAY voo day koohr oh-zhoor-DWEE?

Can I get a tour of the gym?
Puis-je avoir une visite guidée de la salle de sport ?
PWE-zhuh ah-VWAHR ewn VEE-zeet gee-DAY duh la sahl duh spohr?

Where are the lockers located?
Où se trouvent les casiers ?
OO suh TROO-vuh lay kah-SYAY?

How much does it cost to use the gym?
Combien coûte l'utilisation de la salle de sport ?
Kohm-BYAN koot l'yoo-tee-lee-zah-see-yohn duh la sahl duh spohr?

Can I borrow a towel?
Puis-je emprunter une serviette ?
PWE-zhuh ahm-pruhN-tay ewn sair-vyet?

Where is the water fountain?
Où se trouve la fontaine d'eau ?
OO suh TROO-vuh lah fawn-TEN doh?

Do you have any yoga mats?
Avez-vous des tapis de yoga ?
Ah-VAY voo day ta-PEE duh yo-GAH?

Is there a sauna here?
Y a-t-il un sauna ici ?
Ee ah-TEEL uhn SOH-nah ee-see?

How do I use this machine?
Comment utiliser cette machine ?
Koh-mahn oo-tee-lee-zay set MA-sheen?

Can you spot me?
Pouvez-vous m'assister ?
Poo-VAY voo mah-sis-TAY?

Where can I find the dumbbells?
Où puis-je trouver les haltères ?
OO pweezh zhuh troo-VEH lay AHLT-AIR?

Is there a locker room here?
Y a-t-il un vestiaire ici ?
EE ah-TEEL un veh-stee-AIR ee-SEE?

How much does a personal trainer cost?
Combien coûte un entraîneur personnel ?
Kom-bee-ahn koot un ahn-tray-NER pair-so-nel?

Can I use the treadmill?
Puis-je utiliser le tapis roulant ?
Pweezh zhuh oo-tee-lee-ZAY luh tah-PEE roo-LAHN?

Is there a weight limit on the machines?
Y a-t-il une limite de poids sur les machines ?
EE ah-TEEL oon LEE-mit duh pwa sur lay ma-SHEEN?

Can I pay with a credit card?
Puis-je payer par carte de crédit ?
Pweezh zhuh pay-YAY par kart duh kre-DEE?

Where can I find the exercise balls?
Où puis-je trouver les balles d'exercice ?
OO pweezh zhuh troo-VEH lay bal dex-ehr-SEES?

How many reps and sets should I do?
Combien de répétitions et de séries devrais-je faire ?
Kom-bee-ahn duh ray-pay-tee-SYAWN ay duh say-ree dev-ray zhuh fair?

Do you offer group classes?
Proposez-vous des cours en groupe ?
Pro-poh-ZAY voo day koor ahn groop?

Can I bring a friend to the gym?
Puis-je amener un ami au gym ?
Pweezh zhuh ah-muh-NAY run ah-mee oh zhee?

Is there a pool here?
Y a-t-il une piscine ici?
EE-ah-TEEL oon pee-SEEN e-see?

What kind of workouts are you doing today?
Quels types d'exercices faites-vous aujourd'hui?
KELL tee-peh deh-kser-SEES fett-VOO oh-zhoor-DWEE?

Do you have any advice on how to improve my form for this exercise?
Avez-vous des conseils pour améliorer ma forme pour cet exercice?
AH-veh-VOO day kohn-seh-YEE pour ah-meh-lee-or mah form pour set ex-ehr-SEES?

How many sets/reps are you doing for that exercise?
Combien de séries / répétitions faites-vous pour cet exercice?
Kohn-BYEN duh seh-REE / ray-pay-tee-SEE-ohn feh-VOO poor set ex-ehr-SEES?

Would you like to work in with me on this equipment?
Voulez-vous travailler avec moi sur cet équipement?
VOO-leh-VOO trav-eye-yay ah-vek mwah sur set eh-kee-puh-MEHNT?

Do you know how to use this piece of equipment?
Savez-vous comment utiliser cet équipement?
Sah-veh-VOO koh-mahn oo-til-ee-zay set eh-kee-puh-MEHNT?

This exercise is really challenging, but I'm going to push through it.
Cet exercice est vraiment difficile, mais je vais le faire.
Set ex-ehr-SEES eh veh-ray-mahn dee-fee-SEEL, may zhuh vay luh fair.

I like to switch up my workouts to keep things interesting.
J'aime changer mes séances d'entraînement pour que les choses restent intéressantes.
Jah-eem shahn-jay may seh-ahnss dahn-treh-nuh-mahn poor kuh lay shohz ruh-stahn ehn-teh-ray-ess-ahnt.

I need to make an appointment with a doctor.
Je dois prendre rendez-vous avec un médecin.
ZHUH DWAH prahn-druh-VOO ah-vehk uhn meh-DUH-sahn.

How do I find a good doctor in my area?
Comment trouver un bon médecin dans ma région ?
KOH-mahn truh-VEH oon bohn meh-DUH-sahn dahn mah ray-ZHON ?

What do I need to bring to my doctor's appointment?
Que dois-je apporter à mon rendez-vous chez le médecin ?
KUH DWAHZH ah-pohr-TEH ah mohn rahn-day-VOO shay luh meh-DUH-sahn ?

How early should I arrive for my appointment?
À quelle heure dois-je arriver à mon rendez-vous ?
AH KELL UHR DWAHZH ah-ree-VEH ah mohn rahn-day-VOO ?

Where is the doctor's office located?
Où se trouve le cabinet du médecin ?
OO suh troov luh kah-beh-DUH duh meh-DUH-sahn ?

Is there parking available at the doctor's office?
Y a-t-il du stationnement disponible au cabinet du médecin ?
EE ah-TEEL dew stah-syoan-NAH-mahn dah-vee-LAHBL uh kah-beh-DUH duh meh-DUH-sahn ?

Can I bring someone with me to my appointment?
Puis-je amener quelqu'un avec moi à mon rendez-vous ?
POOZH-juh ah-muh-NEH kel-KUH unh vehk MWAH ah mohn rahn-day-VOO ?

How long will I have to wait to see the doctor?
Combien de temps vais-je devoir attendre pour voir le médecin ?
KOH-byah d uh tahng VEHZH duh-VWAHR ah-tahn-druh poor vwahr luh meh-DUH-sahn ?

What if I need to reschedule my appointment?
Et si je dois reprogrammer mon rendez-vous ?
EH see zhuh DWAH ruh-proh-GRAHM-eh mohn rahn-day-VOO ?

How do I cancel my appointment?
Comment annuler mon rendez-vous ?
KOH-mahn ah-nyuh-LEH mohn rahn-day-VOO ?

What do I do if I have an emergency and need to see a doctor immediately?
Que dois-je faire si j'ai une urgence et que j'ai besoin de voir un médecin immédiatement ?
Kuh DWAHZH fayr see zhuh-NUR-jhuh see zhay oo-nuh meh-DUH-sahn ee-MEH-dee-ah-MAHN.

Do I need a referral to see a specialist?
Ai-je besoin d'une référence pour consulter un spécialiste ?
EHZH buh-ZWAH d'yoon REH-feh-RAHNS poor kohn-suhl-TAY uhn speh-see-ah-LEEST.

How much will my appointment cost?
Combien coûtera mon rendez-vous ?
KOH-byah coo-TAY-rah mohn rahn-day-VOO ?

Will my insurance cover the cost of my appointment?
Mon assurance couvrira-t-elle les frais de mon rendez-vous ?
MOHN ah-soo-RAHNS koo-vree-rah-TEHL lay frah duh mohn rahn-day-VOO ?

What forms of payment are accepted at the doctor's office?
Quels sont les moyens de paiement acceptés au cabinet du médecin ?
KEHL sohn lay moh-YAN duh pay-MAHNT ahk-sep-TAY oh kah-beh-DUH duh meh-DUH-sahn ?

Can I request a prescription refill over the phone?
Puis-je demander un renouvellement d'ordonnance par téléphone ?
POOZH-juh dahn-MAN-day uhn ruh-noo-vluh-MUHN dohr-doh-NANS pahr teh-lay-FOHN.

How do I get my test results?
Comment obtenir les résultats de mes examens ?
KOH-mahn ohb-tuh-NEER lay ray-zool-tah duh meh-zah-MUHN ?

Do I need to fast before my appointment?
Dois-je jeûner avant mon rendez-vous ?
DWAZH zhuh zhuh-NAY ah-vahnt mohn rahn-day-VOO ?

Can I eat or drink anything before my appointment?
Puis-je manger ou boire quelque chose avant mon rendez-vous ?
POOZH-juh mahn-ZHAY oo bwahr kuhl-KUH shohz ah-vahnt mohn rahn-day-VOO ?

Do I need to bring my medical records with me to my appointment?
Dois-je apporter mes dossiers médicaux à mon rendez-vous ?
DWAZH zhuh ah-pohr-TEH may doh-see-AYR may-dee-KOH ah mohn rahn-day-VOO ?

Can I access my medical records online?
Puis-je accéder à mes dossiers médicaux en ligne ?
POOZH-juh ahk-say-DAY ah may doh-see-AYR may-dee-KOH ahn LEEN-yuh?

How do I schedule a follow-up appointment?
Comment planifier un rendez-vous de suivi ?
Koh-mahn plah-nee-FYAY uhn rahn-day-VOO duh soo-vee?

How do I get a second opinion?
Comment obtenir un deuxième avis médical ?
Koh-mahn ohb-tuh-NEER uh duh-zhehm AH-vees may-dee-KAL?

What if I have a question after my appointment?
Et si j'ai une question après mon rendez-vous ?
Ay-tee zhay ewn keh-stee-AWN ah-PRAY mohn rahn-day-VOO?

Can I contact my doctor outside of office hours?
Puis-je contacter mon médecin en dehors des heures de bureau ?
POOZH-juh kohn-tahk-TAY mohn may-dee-SAHN ahn duh-OR dayz ur duh buh-ROH?

How do I request a medical certificate for work?

Comment demander un certificat médical pour le travail ?

Koh-mahn duh-mahn-DAY uhn suhr-tee-fee-KAH may-dee-KAL poor luh trah-VYE?

What do I do if I experience side effects from my medication?

Que dois-je faire si je ressens des effets secondaires de mon médicament ?

Kuh DWAHZH fayr see zhuh ruh-SAHN dayz eh-fay suh-gohn-dair duh mohn may-dee-kuh-MAHNT?

How do I know if my symptoms require a visit to the doctor?

Comment savoir si mes symptômes nécessitent une visite chez le médecin ?

Koh-mahn sah-vwahr see may sim-TOHM neh-seh-see-TAHN ewn VEE-zeet shay luh may-dee-SAHN?

How do I prepare for a surgery?

Comment me préparer pour une intervention chirurgicale ?

Koh-mahn muh prey-pah-RAY poor ewn ahn-ter-vahn-see-ohn shee-roo-rjee-KAHL?

What should I expect during a hospital stay?

À quoi dois-je m'attendre pendant mon séjour à l'hôpital ?

Ah kwah DWAHZH muh-tahn-druh pahn-dahn mohn say-ZHOOR ah loh-pee-TAHL?

COMMON GREETINGS

Hello
Bonjour
Bohn-JOOR

Hi/Hey
Salut
Sah-LEW

Good morning
Bonjour (used until around noon)
Bohn-JOOR

Good afternoon
Bonjour (used from noon until evening)
Bohn-JOOR

Good evening
Bonsoir
Bohn-SWAHR

Greetings
Salutations
Sah-loo-TAH-see-ohn

What's up?
Quoi de neuf ?
Kwah duh NUHF

How's it going?
Comment ça va ?
Koh-MOHN sah VAH

How are you doing?
Comment allez-vous ?
Koh-MOHN tah-lay-VOO

Nice to meet you
Enchanté(e)
Ahn-shahn-TAY

Pleasure to meet you
Ravi(e) de vous rencontrer
Rah-vee duh voo rehn-kohn-TRAH

It's good to see you
Ça fait plaisir de vous voir
Sah feh pleh-ZEER duh voo vwar

Long time no see
Ça fait longtemps qu'on ne s'est pas vu(e)(s)
Sah feh lohng-tohn kohn nuh seh pah voo(eye)(z)

Hey, what's going on with you today?
Salut, qu'est-ce qui se passe aujourd'hui ?
Sah-LEW, kehss-kee suh PAHS oh-zhoo-DWEE?

Hi, how's your day going so far?
Salut, comment se passe ta journée jusqu'à présent ?
*SAH-lyoo, koh-MOHN suh PAHS tuh zhoor-NAY zhoo-SKAH
pah-reh-SAHN?*

Good evening, how can I assist you?
Bonsoir, comment puis-je vous aider ?
Bohn-SWAHR, koh-mohn PWEESH zhuh voo zeh-DEH?

Good morning, how are you?
Bonjour, comment allez-vous ?
Bohn-JOOR, koh-mohn tah-LAY voo?

Nice to see you again.
Ravi de vous revoir.
Rah-VEE duh voo ruh-VOIR.

How have you been?
Comment ça va depuis la dernière fois qu'on s'est vu ?
Koh-MOHN sah VAH duh-PUIS lah DAYR-NYAIR fwa kawn seh voo?

What's new?
Quoi de neuf ?
Kwah duh NUHF?

Hey there, how's it going?
Salut, comment ça va ?
SAH-luht, koh-MOHN sah VAH?

Hey there, nice to see you!
Salut, ça fait plaisir de te voir !
SAH-luht, sah FEH pleh-ZEEHR duh tuh vwar!

How's your day going so far?
Comment se passe ta journée jusqu'à présent ?
Koh-MOHN suh PAHS tuh zhoor-NAY zhoo-SKAH pah-reh-SAHN?

What brings you here today?
Qu'est-ce qui vous amène ici aujourd'hui?
Kess-kee voo zah-MEN EE-see oh-zhoor-DWEE?

I hope you're doing well.
J'espère que vous allez bien.
Zhehs-PAIR kuh voo ZAH-lay bee-EN.

Hello, it's great to meet you!
Bonjour, c'est un plaisir de vous rencontrer!
Bohn-ZHOOR, say tun pleh-ZEER duh voo ruhn-kohn-TRAY!

BANKING

I need to deposit this check into my account.
J'ai besoin de déposer ce chèque sur mon compte.
ZHAY buh-ZWAH deh deh-POH-zay suh SHEK sur mohn COHMPT.

Can I withdraw some cash from the ATM?
Est-ce que je peux retirer de l'argent liquide au distributeur automatique ?
ESS-kuh zhuh PUH retihray duh LAHRZHANH lee-KEED oh dee-STREE-byoo-TEUR ah-toh-mah-TEEK?

I want to open a savings account.
Je voudrais ouvrir un compte d'épargne.
ZHUH voo-DRAY oo-VREH uhn COHNT deh-PAHNYE.

What's the interest rate on this loan?
Quel est le taux d'intérêt de ce prêt ?
KELL EH luh toh dahn-teh-RAY duh suh PRAY?

I need to transfer money to another account.
Je dois transférer de l'argent vers un autre compte.
ZHUH dwah trahnz-feh-RAY duh LAHRZHANH ver uhn oh-truh COHMPT.

Can I get a credit card with this bank?
Est-ce que je peux avoir une carte de crédit avec cette banque ?
ESS-kuh zhuh PUH-uh-vwahr oon kahrt duh KRAY-dee ah-vehk suh-SET bonk?

I need to pay my credit card bill.
Je dois payer ma facture de carte de crédit.
ZHUH dwah pay-ayr ma fahk-TOOR duh kahrt duh KRAY-dee.

I want to close my account.
Je veux fermer mon compte.
ZHUH vuh fur-MAY mohn COHMPT.

Can I set up automatic bill payments?
Est-ce que je peux mettre en place des paiements automatiques de
factures ?
*ESS-kuh zhuh PUH met-truh ahn plahs dayz pay-MAHN
oh-toh-mah-TEEK duh fahk-TOOR?*

I need to order checks.
Je dois commander des chèques.
ZHUH dwah koh-mahn-DAY day SHEK.

What's the penalty for early withdrawal?
Quelle est la pénalité pour un retrait anticipé ?
KELL EH lah peh-nah-LEE-TAY poor uh ruh-TRAY ahn-tee-SEE-pay?

Can I get a mortgage with this bank?
Est-ce que je peux obtenir un prêt hypothécaire avec cette banque ?
*ESS-kuh zhuh PUH ohb-teh-NEER uhn PRAY oh-tee-PECK-air ah-vehk
suh-SET bonk?*

I need to apply for a personal loan.
Je dois faire une demande de prêt personnel.
ZHUH dwah fair oon dah-MAHND duh PRAY per-soh-NEHL.

How do I dispute a transaction on my statement?
Comment contester une transaction sur mon relevé bancaire ?
*KOH-mahn kon-teh-STAYR oon trahn-zak-see-YON sur mohn
ruh-luh-VAY bahn-CAIR?*

I want to check my account online.
Je veux vérifier mon compte en ligne.
ZHUH vuh veh-ree-FEE mohn COHMPT ahn leen.

What's the overdraft fee?
Quel est le montant des frais de découvert ?
KELL EH luh mohn-TAHN day fray duh day-koo-VEHR?

How do I set up direct deposit?
Comment mettre en place un dépôt direct ?
KOH-mahn met-truh ahn plahs uhn day-poh dhee-REKT?

Can I get a cashier's check?
Est-ce que je peux obtenir un chèque de banque ?
ESS-kuh zhuh PUH ohb-teh-NEER uhn SHEK duh bonk?

I need to make a wire transfer.
Je dois effectuer un virement bancaire.
ZHUH dwahz eh-fehk-tew-uhr uhn veer-mawn bahn-CAIR.

What's the minimum balance for this account?
Quel est le solde minimum pour ce compte ?
KELL EH luh SOHLD meen-ee-MUHN poor suh COHMT?

I want to set up a joint account.
Je veux ouvrir un compte joint.
ZHUH vuh oo-VREER uhn COHMT zhwan.

How long does it take for a check to clear?
Combien de temps faut-il pour que le chèque soit encaissé ?
KOHM-bee-ahn duh TAHN foh-TEEL poor kuh SHEK swah ohn-kay-SAY?

Can I open a business account?
Est-ce que je peux ouvrir un compte professionnel ?
ESS-kuh zhuh PUH oo-VREER uhn COHMT proh-fess-ee-oh-NELL?

I need to reorder my debit card.
Je dois commander une nouvelle carte de débit.
ZHUH dwah koh-mahn-DAYR oon noo-VEL kart duh day-BEE.

What's the APR on this credit card?
Quel est le taux d'intérêt annuel sur cette carte de crédit ?
KELL EH luh toh dan-teh-RAY ahn-nwell sur suh-set kart duh kray-DEE?

I want to enroll in paperless statements.
Je veux m'inscrire aux relevés sans papier.
ZHUH vuh mawn-skreew oh ruh-luh-VAY sahn pah-PYAY.

Can I set up a savings plan?
Est-ce que je peux mettre en place un plan d'épargne ?
ESS-kuh zhuh PUH met-truh ahn plahs uh plahn day-pahn-YEHN?

What's the foreign transaction fee?
Quel est le montant des frais de transaction à l'étranger ?
KELL EH luh mohn-tahn day fray duh trahn-zak-see-YOHN ah lay-trahn-ZHAY?

How do I change my account information?
Comment modifier les informations de mon compte ?
KOH-mahn moh-dee-FEE-ay lay zihn-fohr-mah-see-YOHN duh mohn COHMT?

What's my account balance?
Quel est le solde de mon compte ?
KELL EH luh SOHL-duh duh mohn COHMPT?

COMMON TRAVELER QUESTIONS

How do I get to the airport/train station/bus station?
Comment puis-je me rendre à l'aéroport/à la gare routière/à la gare ?
KOH-mahng pweezh zhuh muh rahndruh ah lair-oh-PORT/ah lah gahr roo-TYAIR/ah lah gahr?

What time does the next train/bus/plane leave?
À quelle heure part le prochain train/bus/avion ?
AH kehl uhr pahr luh proh-SHANG trang/boos/ahv-YOHN?

How much does it cost to take a taxi to my hotel?
Combien coûte un taxi pour aller à mon hôtel ?
KOHNG-bee-ang koot uh tahk-SEE poor ah-lay ah mohn ho-TELL?

Can you recommend a good hotel/hostel?
Pouvez-vous me recommander un bon hôtel/une bonne auberge de jeunesse ?
POO-vay-VOO muh ruh-koh-mahn-DAY uhng bohn ho-TELL/oohn bohn OH-bairj duh juh-NESS?

What is the best way to get around the city?
Quel est le meilleur moyen de se déplacer dans la ville ?
KELL ay luh muh-YEUR mwahng duh suh day-plah-SAY dahn lah VEEL?

Is there a shuttle bus from the airport to the city center?
Y a-t-il une navette de l'aéroport jusqu'au centre-ville ?
EE-yah-TEEL ewn nuh-VET duh lair-oh-PORT zhoo-skooh oh SAHNGT-veel?

How do I buy a ticket for the public transportation system?
Comment acheter un billet pour le système de transport public ?
KOH-mahng oh-SHAY un bee-YAY poor luh SEES-tehm duh trahns-pohr poo-BLEEK?

What are some must-see tourist attractions in the area?

Quelles sont les attractions touristiques à ne pas manquer dans la région ?

KEHL sohn lay ah-trahk-see-YOHN toor-EE-stEEK ah nuh pah mahn-KAY dahn lah ray-zh-YOHNG?

Where can I find a good restaurant?

Où puis-je trouver un bon restaurant ?

OO pwis zhuh truh-VAY uh bohn reh-stoh-RAHNG?

Can you recommend a local dish to try?

Pouvez-vous me recommander un plat local à essayer ?

POO-vay-VOO muh ruh-koh-mahn-DAY uh plah loh-KAHL ah ess-AY-yay?

How do I say thank you in the local language?

Comment dit-on merci dans la langue locale ?

KOH-mahng dee-TAWN mair-SEE dahn lah lahng lok-AHL?

What is the weather like today/this week?

Quel temps fait-il aujourd'hui/cette semaine ?

KELL tahng feh-TEEL oh-zhoor-DWEE/set SEM-ahn?

Can you tell me more about the local culture?

Pouvez-vous me parler davantage de la culture locale ?

POO-vay-VOO muh pahr-LAY dah-vahngtahzh duh lah kool-TOOR lok-AHL?

How much should I tip at restaurants?

Combien devrais-je laisser de pourboire dans les restaurants ?

KOHNG-bee-ang duh-vrehzh zhuh leh-SAY duh poor-BWAHR dahn lay roh-stoh-RAHNG?

Is it safe to walk around at night in this area?

Est-ce sûr de se promener la nuit dans cette région ?

ESS suh SUR duh suh proh-muh-NAY lah nwee dahn SET reh-zhee-YOHNG?

How do I access the internet while I'm here?
Comment puis-je accéder à Internet pendant mon séjour ici ?
KOH-mahng pweezh zhuh ah-seh-DAY ah in-tair-NEHT pahn-dahn mohn say-ZHOOR ee-see?

Can I pay with a credit card here?
Puis-je payer avec une carte de crédit ici ?
POUIS-JUH pay-YAY ah-vehk ewn kahrt duh KRAY-deet ee-see?

Where can I exchange currency?
Où puis-je échanger de la monnaie ?
OO pwis zhuh ey-shahng-ZHAY duh lah moh-NAY?

Is it customary to haggle when shopping at local markets?
Est-ce habituel de marchander lors des achats dans les marchés locaux ?
ESS suh ah-bee-TUEHL duh mar-shahn-DAY lohr dayz ah-SHAH dahn lay mar-SHAY lok-OH?

What is the local time here?
Quelle heure est-il ici ?
KEHL uhr ess-TEEL ee-see?

How do I call a taxi?
Comment appeler un taxi ?
KOH-mahng ah-puh-LAY ung tahk-SEE?

Is there a pharmacy nearby?
Y a-t-il une pharmacie à proximité ?
EE ah-TEEL ewn fahr-mah-SEE ah prok-SEE-mee-TAY?

Can you recommend a good place to go for a hike?
Pouvez-vous recommander un bon endroit pour faire de la randonnée ?
POO-vay-VOO ruh-kuh-mahn-DAY ung bohn ahn-DWAA pohr fair duh lah rahn-doh-NAY?

Are there any festivals or events happening during my visit?

Y a-t-il des festivals ou des événements qui se déroulent pendant ma visite ?

EE ah-TEEL day fes-tee-VAHL oo dayz ay-veh-NAHM kee suh day-roo-LUH pahn-dahn mahn vee-ZEET?

How do I get to the nearest beach/park/museum?

Comment puis-je me rendre à la plage/au parc/au musée le plus proche ?

KOH-mahng pweezh zhuh muh rahn-druh ah lah plahzh/oh park/oh myoo-ZAY luh ploh prohsh?

Is there a dress code for visiting religious sites?

Y a-t-il un code vestimentaire à respecter pour visiter les sites religieux ?

EE ah-TEEL ung kohd vay-stee-mahn-TAIR ah ruh-spehk-tay pohr vee-zee-tay lay seet ruh-lee-zhee-uh?

How do I book a guided tour?

Comment réserver une visite guidée ?

KOH-mahng ray-ser-VAY oon vee-ZEET gee-DAY?

What is the local public transportation schedule?

Quel est l'horaire des transports en commun locaux ?

KELL ess loh-RAY duh trahn-spor-tahn koh-MUHN loh-KOH?

Can you recommend a good place to go shopping?

Pouvez-vous recommander un bon endroit pour faire du shopping ?

POO-vay-VOO ruh-kuh-mahn-DAY ung bohn ahn-DWAA pohr fair doo shoh-PEENG?

Where can I find a map of the area?

Où puis-je trouver une carte de la région ?

OO pwis zhuh troo-VAY ewn kahrt duh lah ray-ZHOHNG?

DESCRIBING JOBS AND PROFESSIONS

I work in the tech industry.
Je travaille dans l'industrie technologique.
ZHuh trah-VA-yuh dahn lah[n] DEES-tree teh-nuh-loh-ZHEEK.

I'm a lawyer.
Je suis avocat(e).
ZHuh swee AH-voh-KAH(t).

I'm a doctor.
Je suis médecin.
ZHuh swee may-duh-SAN.

I'm a teacher.
Je suis enseignant(e).
ZHuh swee ah[n]-seh-NYAH(n).

I'm an accountant.
Je suis comptable.
ZHuh swee koh[n]-TAH-bluh.

I'm an engineer.
Je suis ingénieur(e).
ZHuh swee ah[n]-zheh-nyeur.

I work in finance.
Je travaille dans la finance.
ZHuh trah-VA-yuh dahn lah[n] fih-NAHNS.

I'm a journalist.
Je suis journaliste.
ZHuh swee zhoor-nah-LEEST.

I'm a musician.
Je suis musicien(ne).
ZHuh swee moo-zee-SYEH(n).

I'm an artist.
Je suis artiste.
ZHuh swee ahr-TEEST.

I'm a chef.
Je suis chef.
ZHuh swee SHEF.

I work in marketing.
Je travaille dans le marketing.
Juh trah-VEYE dahn luh mar-ke-ting.

I'm a salesperson.
Je suis un vendeur/une vendeuse.
Juh swee uh ven-DUHR/ewn ven-DUHZ.

I'm a software developer.
Je suis un développeur/une développeuse de logiciels.
Juh swee uh day-veh-loh-PUR/ewn day-veh-loh-PURZ duh loh-gi-see-yel.

I work in customer service.
Je travaille dans le service client.
Juh trah-VEYE dahn luh ser-vees klee-yaht.

I'm a graphic designer.
Je suis un designer graphique/une designeuse graphique.
Juh swee uh dee-zeen-EHR grah-fee-k/ewn dee-zeen-UHZ grah-fee-k.

I'm a writer.
Je suis un écrivain/une écrivaine.
Juh swee uh ay-kree-VAN/ewn ay-kree-VEN.

I'm a consultant.
Je suis un consultant/une consultante.
Juh swee uh kohn-sul-TAHNT/ewn kohn-sul-TAHNT.

I work in human resources.
Je travaille dans les ressources humaines.
Juh trah-VEYE dahn lay ruh-SOORS yew-mehn.

I'm a project manager.
Je suis un chef de projet/une cheffe de projet.
Juh swee uh shef duh pro-JE/ewn shef duh pro-JE.

I'm a social worker.
Je suis un travailleur social/une travailleuse sociale.
Juh swee uh trah-vah-YEUR so-see-YAL/ewn trah-vah-YEUZ so-see-YAL.

I work in public relations.
Je travaille dans les relations publiques.
Juh trah-VEYE dahn lay ruh-la-see-YOH(n) poo-bleek.

I'm a nurse.
Je suis un infirmier/une infirmière.
Juh swee uh an-feer-MYAY/ewn an-feer-MYEHR.

I'm a scientist.
Je suis un scientifique/une scientifique.
Juh swee uh san-tee-feeK/ewn san-tee-feeK.

I'm a researcher.
Je suis un chercheur/une chercheuse.
Juh swee uh shair-shur/ewn shair-shUHZ.

I'm a therapist.
Je suis un thérapeute/une thérapeute.
Juh swee uh tay-rah-PUR-t/ewn tay-rah-PUR-t.

I work in hospitality.
Je travaille dans l'hôtellerie.
JUH trah-VAI dahn lo-tell-uh-REE.

I'm a real estate agent.
Je suis agent immobilier.
JUH swee ah-ZHAN ee-moh-bee-LYAY.

I'm a financial advisor.
Je suis conseiller financier.
JUH swee kohn-say-YAY fin-an-see-YAY.

I'm a pharmacist.
Je suis pharmacien(ne).
JUH swee far-mah-see-YEN(NE).

What do you do for a living?
Que faites-vous dans la vie?
Kuh FAYT-voo dahn la vee?

What kind of work do you do?
Quel genre de travail faites-vous?
KELL zhahn-ruh duh trah-VYAH fayt-voo?

Can you describe your job?
Pouvez-vous décrire votre travail?
Poo-VAY voo day-KREER voh-truh trah-VYAH?

What are your main duties and responsibilities?
Quelles sont vos principales fonctions et responsabilités?
*KELL sohn voh prayn-SEE-pahl fonk-see-YOHn ay
ray-spon-sah-bee-LAY?*

What kind of skills and qualifications are required for your job?
Quels sont les compétences et les qualifications requises pour votre
travail?
*KELL sohn lay kohn-puh-TAHNS ay lay kwal-ee-fee-KAH-syon ruh-KEEZ
pour vo-truh trah-VYAH?*

What do you like about your job?
Qu'est-ce que vous aimez dans votre travail?
KESS-kuh voo ZEH-may dahn vo-truh trah-VYAH?

What do you find challenging about your job?
Qu'est-ce que vous trouvez difficile dans votre travail?
KESS-kuh voo troo-VAY dee-fee-SEEL dahn vo-truh trah-VYAH?

How long have you been working in this field?
Depuis combien de temps travaillez-vous dans ce domaine?
*Duh-PWEE kohm-BYEN duh tah(n) trah-vah-YAY voo dahn suh
doh-MEHN?*

What made you choose this profession?
Qu'est-ce qui vous a fait choisir cette profession?
KESS-kee voo ah fay shwah-ZEER suh-tah pro-fes-yohn?

COMMON RESPONSES TO QUESTIONS

Yes
Oui
Whee

No
Non
Nohn

Maybe
Peut-être
Puht-ETR

I don't know
Je ne sais pas
Zhuh nuh say pah

That's possible
C'est possible
Say pos-SEE-bluh

That's impossible
C'est impossible
Say im-POS-see-bluh

I agree
Je suis d'accord
Zhuh swee dah-KOR

I disagree
Je ne suis pas d'accord
Zhuh nuh swee pah dah-KOR

I understand
Je comprends
Zhuh kohn-PRAH

I don't understand
Je ne comprends pas
Zhuh nuh kohn-PRAH pah

Could you repeat that, please?
Pourriez-vous répéter, s'il vous plaît?
Pooh-ree-eh voo ray-PAY-teh, SEEL VOUS PLAIT?

Can you explain that in more detail?
Pouvez-vous expliquer cela plus en détail?
Poo-veh voo ehk-plee-kay suh-LAH plew zahn day-TA-ee?

Let me think about it
Laissez-moi y réfléchir
LEH-seh-mwah ee ray-FLEH-sheer

Let me get back to you on that
Je reviendrai vers vous à ce sujet
Zhuh ruh-vee-ehn-DRAY vehr VOO ah suh suh-ZHAY

I'm not sure
Je ne suis pas sûre
Zhuh nuh swee pah syoor

It depends
Cela dépend
Suh-LAH day-PAHN

Absolutely
Absolument
Ab-soh-LOO-mahn

Not at all
Pas du tout
Pah dew too

Of course
Bien sûr
Bee-ehn soor

Definitely
Certainement
Sair-tahn-MAN

Absolutely not
Absolument pas
Ab-soh-LOO-mahn pah

That's a good point
C'est une bonne remarque
Say oo-nuh bohn ruh-MARK

That's a fair point
C'est une remarque juste
Say oo-nuh ruh-MARK zhuhst

That's an interesting point
C'est une remarque intéressante
Say oo-nuh ruh-MARK ahn-teh-reh-SAHnt

I appreciate your input
Je vous remercie pour votre contribution
Zhuh voo ruh-mair-SEE poor voh-truh kohn-trih-byoo-see-ohn

Thank you for asking
Merci de demander
Mehr-SEE duh doh-MAHN-day

I'm sorry, I can't answer that
Je suis désolée, je ne peux pas répondre à cela
Zhuh swee day-zoh-LEH, zhuh nuh puh pah reh-POHn-dr ah suh-LAH

I'm not the best person to ask about that
Je ne suis pas la meilleure personne à qui demander à ce sujet
Zhuh nuh swee pah lah muh-yehr pehr-SOHN ah kee doh-MAHN-day ah suh suh-ZHAY

That's not my area of expertise
Ce n'est pas mon domaine de compétence
Suh neh pah mohn doh-MEN duh kohm-peh-TAHns

That's beyond my knowledge
Cela dépasse mes connaissances
Suh-LAH day-PAHS meh koh-nuh-SAHNS

Dog
Chien
Shee-EN

Cat
Chat
Sha

Bird
Oiseau
Wah-zoh

Fish
Poisson
Pwah-SON

Hamster
Hamster
Ahm-stair

Guinea pig
Cobaye
Koh-bye

Rabbit
Lapin
Lah-pahn

Ferret
Furet
Fyoo-ray

Hedgehog
Hérisson
Ay-ree-SON

Chinchilla
Chinchilla
Sheen-shee-lah

Mouse
Souris
Soo-REE

Rat
Rat
Rah

Gerbil
Gerbille
Zhehr-beel

Snake
Serpent
Sair-PAHNT

Lizard
Lézard
LEH-zahr

Tortoise
Tortue
TOR-tew

Hermit crab
Bernard-l'ermite
BEHR-nahr lehr-MEET

Tarantula
Tarantule
TAH-rahn-tewl

Scorpion
Scorpion
Skohr-PEE-ohn

Bearded dragon
Dragon barbu
DRAH-gohn bahr-BYU

Pot-bellied pig
Cochon nain
Koh-SHOH nahn

Miniature horse
Cheval miniature
Shuh-VAHL mee-nee-ah-TUHR

Goat
Chèvre
SHEV-ruh

Sheep
Mouton
Moo-TAWN

Chicken
Poulet
Poo-LAY

Duck
Canard
Kah-NAHR

What kind of pets do you have?
Quels types d'animaux de compagnie avez-vous?
KELL TEEP dan-ee-MO duh kohn-pah-NYEH ah-veh-VOO?

Do you have any tips for training a new pet?
Avez-vous des conseils pour entraîner un nouvel animal de compagnie?
AH-veh-VOO day kohn-seh-EE pohr ahn-tray-NAY ahn noo-VEL an-ee-mahl duh kohn-pah-NYEH?

What is your favorite thing about your pet?
Quelle est votre chose préférée à propos de votre animal de compagnie?
KELL EH voh-truh shohz pray-FAIR-ay ah PRO-poh duh voh-truh
an-ee-mahl duh kohn-pah-NYEH?

Have you ever adopted a pet from a shelter?
Avez-vous déjà adopté un animal de compagnie d'un refuge?
AH-veh-VOO day-zhah ah-dop-TAY uh an-ee-mahl duh kohn-pah-NYEH
duh ruh-FYUZH?

What is your pet's name?
Comment s'appelle votre animal de compagnie?
Koh-MOHN sah-PELL voh-truh an-ee-mahl duh kohn-pah-NYEH?

How do you keep your pet healthy?
Comment maintenez-vous votre animal de compagnie en bonne
santé?
Koh-mahn meh-ten-EH-veh voh-truh ah-nee-MAL duh kohn-PAN-yee
ahn bohn SAWN-teh?

Do you have any funny or heartwarming pet stories to share?
Avez-vous des histoires amusantes ou émouvantes à partager à propos
de votre animal de compagnie?
Ah-veh-VOO dayz ee-STWAHR ah-myoo-ZAHNT oo ay-moo-VAHNT ah
pahr-TAH-zhuh ah proh-POH duh voh-truh ah-nee-MAL duh
kohn-PAN-yee?

What is your opinion on spaying or neutering pets?
Quel est votre avis sur la stérilisation des animaux de compagnie?
Kel eh voh-truh ah-VEE soo-r lah stair-ee-lee-ZA-syohn dayz
ah-nee-MOH duh kohn-PAN-yee?

Have you ever had to say goodbye to a pet?
Avez-vous déjà dû dire au revoir à un animal de compagnie?
Ah-veh-VOO day-ZHAH doo dee oh ruh-VWAH ah uh ah-nee-MAL duh
kohn-PAN-yee?

I love spending time with my pet.
J'adore passer du temps avec mon animal de compagnie.
Zhah-DOHR pah-SAY doo tohn ah-vehk mohn ah-nee-MAL duh kohn-PAN-yee.

COLORS

Red
Rouge
ROOJ

Blue
Bleu
BLUH

Green
Vert
VAYR

Yellow
Jaune
ZHAWN

Orange
Orange
OH-RAHNGZH

Purple
Violet
VYOH-let

Pink
Rose
ROHZ

Brown
Marron
MAH-rohn

Black
Noir
NWAR

White
Blanc
BLAHNK

Gray
Gris
GREE

Navy
Marine
Mah-REEN

Turquoise
Turquoise
TUHR-koiz

Olive
Olive
Oh-LEEV

Teal
Sarcelle
Sahr-SELL

Lavender
Lavande
Lah-VAHND

Beige
Beige
BAYZH

Cyan
Cyan
See-AHN

Salmon
Saumon
Soh-MOHN

Gold
Or
OR

Silver
Argent
Ar-ZHAHN

Bronze
Bronze
BROHNZ

Indigo
Indigo
EHN-dee-goh

Fuchsia
Fuchsia
FYU-sha

Charcoal
Charbon
Shar-BOHN

Peach
Pêche
PESH

Mint
Menthe
MAHNT

Ivory
Ivoire
EE-vwar

Burgundy
Bordeaux
Bohr-DOH

Olive green
Vert olive
Vayr oh-LEEV

What's your favorite color?
Quelle est votre couleur préférée?
KEHL eh vo-tre koo-luhr PREH-feh-reh?

Do you like bright colors or muted ones?
Aimez-vous les couleurs vives ou les couleurs sourdes?
EH-may-voo lay koo-luhr veev or lay koo-luhr soord?

Which color do you think represents happiness?
Quelle couleur pensez-vous qui représente le bonheur?
KEHL koo-luhr PAHNS-ay-voo kee ray-preh-zahnt luh boh-nuhr?

Which color do you think represents sadness?
Quelle couleur pensez-vous qui représente la tristesse?
KEHL koo-luhr PAHNS-ay-voo kee ray-preh-zahnt lah tree-stess?

What color are your eyes?
De quelle couleur sont vos yeux?
Duh KEHL koo-luhr sohn vo zyuh?

Do you prefer warm colors or cool colors?
Préférez-vous les couleurs chaudes ou les couleurs froides?
Preh-feh-ray-voo lay koo-luhr shohd oo lay koo-luhr fwahd?

NUMBERS

One
Un
Uh

Two
Deux
Duh

Three
Trois
Twah

Four
Quatre
KAH-truh

Five
Cinq
Sank

Six
Six
Sees

Seven
Sept
Seht

Eight
Huit
Wheat

Nine
Neuf
Nuhf

Ten
Dix
Dees

Eleven
Onze
Onz

Twelve
Douze
Dooz

Thirteen
Treize
Trehz

Fourteen
Quatorze
Kah-TORZ

Fifteen
Quinze
Kans

Sixteen
Seize
Says

Seventeen
Dix-sept
Dees-SEHT

Eighteen
Dix-huit
Dees-WHEET

Nineteen
Dix-neuf
Dees-NUHF

Twenty
Vingt
Van

Thank you.
Merci.
MEHR-see.

Excuse me, please.
Excusez-moi, s'il vous plaît.
Eks-kyoo-zay MWAH, seel voo play.

I'm sorry.
Je suis désolé(e).
Juh swee day-zoh-LAY.

Please.
S'il vous plaît.
Seel voo play.

May I help you?
Puis-je vous aider?
Pwee zhuh voo zeh-dey?

Nice to meet you.
Enchanté(e).
On-shan-TAY.

Have a good day/evening.
Bonne journée/soirée.
Bohn zhur-NAY/swha-RAY.

After you.
Après vous.
Ah-PRAY voo.

Pardon me.
Excusez-moi.
Eks-kyoo-zay MWAH.

Thank you for your help.
Merci pour votre aide.
MEHR-see poor vo-truh AYD.

May I?
Est-ce que je peux?
Ess-kuh zhuh puh?

Could you?
Pourriez-vous?
Poor-ree-ay voo?

Would you mind?
Est-ce que cela vous dérange?
Ess-kuh suh-lah voo day-rawnzh?

I'm sorry.
Je suis désolé(e).
Juh swee day-zoh-LAY.

Go ahead.
Allez-y.
Ah-lay-ZEE.

No problem.
Pas de problème.
Pah duh pro-BLEHM.

It was my pleasure.
C'était un plaisir.
Say-TAY uh pleh-ZEER.

My apologies.
Mes excuses.
May zeks-KYUZ.

With all due respect.
Avec tout le respect que je vous dois.
Ah-vek too luh ruh-speh KUH zhuh voo dwah.

If you don't mind.
Si cela ne vous dérange pas.
See suh-LAH nuh voo day-rawnzh pah.

If it's not too much trouble.
Si ce n'est pas trop vous demander.
See suh neh pah troh voo duh-MAHN-day.

Thank you kindly.
Merci beaucoup.
MEHR-see boh-KOO.

You're welcome.
De rien.
Duh ree-AN.

No, thank you.
Non, merci.
Noh, MEHR-see.

If I may ask...
Si je peux me permettre de vous demander...
See zhuh puh muh-PAIR-truh duh voo duh-MAHN-day.

If I may add...
Si je peux ajouter...
See zhuh puh za-JOO-tay.

Thank you for your time.
Merci pour votre temps.
MEHR-see poor vo-truh tohn.

It's been a pleasure.
Ce fut un plaisir.
Suh fyuh uh pleh-ZEER.

I appreciate it.
Je vous en suis reconnaissant(e).
Zhuh vooz ah swee ruh-koh-nay-SAHNT.

I'll be happy to help.
Je serai ravi(e) de vous aider.
Zhuh suh-RAY ra-vee duh voo zeh-DAY.

That's very kind of you.
C'est très gentil de votre part.
Say tray zhuhn-TEEL duh vuh-truh PAHR.

Thank you in advance.
Merci d'avance.
MEHR-see dah-VAHNS.

Excuse me for interrupting.
Excusez-moi de vous interrompre.
Ehk-skew-ZAY mwah duh voo zehn-teh-RAWMPR.

I appreciate your help.
J'apprécie votre aide.
Zhah-pree-see vuh-truh ed.

Please let me know.
Faites-moi savoir, s'il vous plaît.
FAYT mwah sah-VWAR, seel voo play.

May I ask a question?
Puis-je poser une question ?
Pwee zhuh po-SAY ewn kest-YAWN.

Could you repeat that, please?
Pouvez-vous répéter, s'il vous plaît ?
Poo-vey voo ray-PAY-tay, seel voo play.

Would you be so kind as to...
Pourriez-vous avoir la gentillesse de...
Poor-ree-ey voo ah-VWAR lah zhuhn-TEEL-ness duh...

I'm sorry to bother you.
Je suis désolé(e) de vous déranger.
Zhuh swee day-zoh-LAY duh voo day-RAHN-jay.

After you, please.
Après vous, je vous en prie.
Ah-PRAY voo, zhuh voo zahN-PREE.

Thank you for your understanding.
Merci pour votre compréhension.
MEHR-see poor vuh-truh kohm-pray-awn-see-ohn.

No, thank you, I'm good.
Non, merci, ça va.
Noh, MEHR-see, sah vah.

Please, take a seat.
Asseyez-vous, s'il vous plaît.
Ah-seh-yay voo, seel voo play.

I'll do my best.
Je ferai de mon mieux.
Zhuh fuh-RAY duh mawn myuh.

Thank you for your patience
Merci pour votre patience
MEHR-see poor vo-truh pah-tee-ahns

May I offer you something to drink?
Puis-je vous offrir quelque chose à boire?
PweeZH voo zawf-REER kel-kuh shohz ah bwahr?

Would you like me to help you?
Voulez-vous que je vous aide?
Voo-lay-VOO kuh zhuh voo ZED?

I beg your pardon, I didn't catch that
Je vous demande pardon, je n'ai pas compris cela
Zhuh voo dom-AHN pahr-DON, zhuh nay pah kom-pree-suh suh-lah

If it's not too much trouble
Si cela ne vous dérange pas trop
See suh-lah nuh voo deh-RAHNZH pah troh

Thank you for your hospitality
Merci pour votre hospitalité
MEHR-see poor vo-truh oh-spee-tah-lee-tay

That's very generous of you
C'est très généreux de votre part
Say tray zheh-nay-ruh de vo-truh pahr

Please accept my apologies
Veuillez accepter mes excuses
Vuh-lay ahk-sep-TAY mayz ehks-KYUZ

If I may make a suggestion...
Si je peux me permettre une suggestion...
See zhuh peuh muh-pair-MEHT-truh oon suh-jes-TYON

I'm sorry, I didn't mean to
Je suis désolé, je n'ai pas voulu
Zhuh swee day-zoh-LAY, zhuh nay pah voo-LOO

Thank you for taking the time
Merci d'avoir pris le temps
MEHR-see da-vwahr pree luh tah

May I offer you a hand?
Puis-je vous donner un coup de main?
PweeZH voo doh-nay uh koo duh mah(n)

My apologies for the inconvenience
Mes excuses pour le dérangement
Mayz ehks-KYUZ poor luh day-RAHNZH-mahn

Please forgive me
S'il vous plaît, pardonnez-moi
Seel voo pleh, pahr-doh-NAY mwah

Thank you for your time and attention
Merci pour votre temps et votre attention
MEHR-see poor vo-truh tah(n) ay vo-truh ah-tahn-syon

It was nice meeting you
C'était un plaisir de vous rencontrer
Say-TAY uhn pleh-ZEER duh voo rehn-kon-TRAY

Excuse me, would you happen to know...?
Excusez-moi, sauriez-vous...?
Eks-KYU-zay mwah, soh-ruh-YAY-voo...?

HANDLING A RUDE PERSON

I would appreciate it if you could speak to me with more respect.
J'apprécierais que vous puissiez me parler avec plus de respect.
ZHAP-REH-SEE-RAY kuh voo POU-SEE-YAY muh par-LAY ah-VEK ploo duh reh-SPEH.

I'm not sure why you're speaking to me like that, but please stop.
Je ne suis pas sûre de pourquoi vous me parlez ainsi, mais s'il vous plaît arrêtez.
ZHUH nuh SWEE pah SURE duh pour-KWAH voo muh par-LAY ah-SEE-zee, may SEEL VOUS PLAIT ah-REH-TAY.

Your behavior is not acceptable.
Votre comportement n'est pas acceptable.
VOH-truh kohn-POR-tuh-MANG neh pah ahk-SEP-tahbl.

I understand that you may be frustrated, but please do not take it out on me.
Je comprends que vous soyez frustrée, mais s'il vous plaît ne le prenez pas sur moi.
ZHUH kohn-PRAHNG keh voo SWAH-yay froo-streh, may SEEL VOUS PLAIT nuh luh PREH-neh pah sur mwah.

Can we please have a respectful conversation?
Pouvons-nous avoir une conversation respectueuse, s'il vous plaît ?
POO-vohn noo ah-VWAHR oon kon-ver-sah-see-YONG res-pek-TUH, SEEL VOUS PLAIT?

I am not willing to tolerate rude behavior.
Je ne suis pas disposée à tolérer un comportement impoli.
ZHUH nuh SWEE pah dees-poh-ZAY ah toh-LEH-reh uh kohn-POR-tuh-MANG ahm-POH-lee.

Please refrain from speaking to me in that manner.
Veuillez vous abstenir de me parler ainsi.
VUH-yay voo zaab-TEH-neer duh muh par-LAY ah-SEE.

It's important to communicate with respect.

Il est important de communiquer avec respect.

EEL eh-tahng-POR-tahn duh koh-moo-nee-KAY ah-vek reh-SPEH.

I will not engage with you if you continue to be rude.

Je ne vais pas continuer à discuter avec vous si vous continuez à être impolie.

ZHUH nuh VAY pah kon-tee-NU-ay ah dee-skoo-TAY ah-vek voo see voo kon-tee-NU-ay ah eht-tuh ahm-POH-lee.

I deserve to be treated with kindness and respect.

Je mérite d'être traitée avec gentillesse et respect.

ZHUH may-REET deh-treh tray-TEH ah-vek zhawn-tee-NESS ay reh-SPEH.

Let's try to resolve this issue without any disrespect.

Essayons de résoudre ce problème sans manque de respect.

EH-seh-YON duh reh-SOO-druh suh PRO-blehm sahn mahnk duh reh-SPEH.

Please choose your words carefully when speaking to me.

S'il vous plaît, choisissez vos mots avec précaution lorsque vous me parlez.

SEEL VOUS PLAIT, shwah-SEE-YAY voh moh ah-VEK prey-koh-SEE-ohn lor-SKuh voo muh par-LAY.

I'm open to listening to your perspective, but please communicate it respectfully.

Je suis prête à écouter votre point de vue, mais veuillez le communiquer avec respect.

ZHUH swee PREH-tah-KOO-tay voh-truh pwan duh vu, may VUH-yay luh koh-moo-nee-KAY ah-vek reh-SPEH.

There's no need to be rude in this situation.

Il n'y a pas besoin d'être impoli dans cette situation.

EEL nee ah pah be-SWAHN deh-treh ahm-POH-lee dahn seht swah-tee-YONG.

I won't allow myself to be treated disrespectfully.
Je ne permettrai pas que l'on me traite avec irrespect.
ZHUH nuh pehr-MEH-tray pah kuh lohn muh TRAYT ah-vek eer-reh-SPEHK.

I'm happy to have a conversation, but only if it's respectful.
Je suis heureux/heureuse de discuter, mais seulement si c'est respectueux.
ZHUH swee uhr-ROO/uhr-ROOZ duh dee-skoo-TAY, may suhl-mahn see say reh-spehk-TEU.

We can communicate effectively without being rude to each other.
Nous pouvons communiquer efficacement sans nous manquer de respect.
NOO poo-vohn koh-moo-nee-KAY eh-fee-kah-suh-MAHN sahn noo mahn-kay duh reh-SPEH.

Please treat me with the same respect that you expect from me.
Veuillez me traiter avec le même respect que celui que vous attendez de moi.
VUH-yay muh TRAY-ter ah-VEK luh mem reh-SPEH kuh suh-LEE kuh voo za-tahn-DAY duh mwah.

Your tone is not appropriate for this conversation.
Votre ton n'est pas approprié pour cette conversation.
VOH-truh tohn neh pah ah-pro-preeh POUR seht kon-ver-sah-see-YONG.

I don't appreciate being spoken to in that manner.
Je n'apprécie pas qu'on me parle de cette manière.
ZHUH nah-PREH-see pah kohn lohn muh PARL duh SET may-NEHR.

I'm willing to discuss this further, but only if you can do so respectfully.
Je suis prête à discuter de cela davantage, mais seulement si vous pouvez le faire avec respect.
Zhuh swee PARE ay dee-SKOO-tay duh suh-LAH, may sewl-mehn see voo puh-vay luh fair ah-vek ruh-spek

You're entitled to your opinion, but please express it respectfully.
Vous avez le droit à votre opinion, mais s'il vous plaît, exprimez-vous avec respect.
Voo ah-VAY luh dwah ah vo-TR pah-nyon, may see voo pleh, eks-preh-may voo ah-vek ruh-spek

It's important to maintain a level of professionalism when communicating.
Il est important de maintenir un niveau de professionnalisme lors de la communication.
Eel eh-tan port-tan duh mahn-teh-NEER uhn nee-VOH duh proh-fess-ee-oh-nah-lizm lor duh la koh-mewn-ee-kah-see-yohn

Please refrain from using offensive language.
Veuillez éviter d'utiliser un langage offensant.
Vuh-LAY zay-vee-tay dew-tee-lee-zay un lan-gaj oh-fawn-sahn

AT THE DOCTOR

Hello, I'm here for my appointment.
Bonjour, je suis là pour mon rendez-vous.
Bohn-ZHOOR, zhuh swee lah poor mohn rahn-d-voo.

I've been experiencing some health problems lately.
J'ai eu quelques problèmes de santé récemment.
Zhay uh KEHLK pro-BLEM duh SAHNT ray-suh-MAHNG.

I would like to schedule an appointment with the doctor.
Je voudrais prendre rendez-vous avec le médecin.
Zhuh voo-DREH prahnd-ruh-voo ah-VEK luh meh-deh-SAN
.

I'm feeling quite unwell.
Je me sens très malade.
Zhuh muh sahN tray ma-LAHD.

I need a check-up.
J'ai besoin d'un examen de contrôle.
Zhay buh-ZWAH duhN ehgz-ah-MUH(N) duh kohn-TROL.

I have some concerns about my health.
J'ai quelques inquiétudes concernant ma santé.
Zhay kehlk a(N)-kee-eh-TEW koh(n)-ser-NAH(n) mah sah(n)-TEH.

I've been experiencing some pain in my [body part].
J'ai ressenti de la douleur dans [ ].
Zh'ay reh-sohn-tee duh lah doo-luhr dahN [ ].

I need a referral to see a specialist.
J'ai besoin d'une référence pour voir un spécialiste.
Zhay buh-ZWAH(N) duh(n) ruh-FEH-re(n)ss poor vwahr u(n) speh-shee-ah-LEEST.

I'm here for a follow-up appointment.
Je suis là pour un rendez-vous de suivi.
Zhuh swee lah poor uhN rahN-day-voo duh soo-VEE.

I'm here for a second opinion.
Je suis là pour un deuxième avis.
Zhuh swee lah poor u(n) duhzy-em AH-vee.

I need to renew my prescription.
J'ai besoin de renouveler mon ordonnance.
ZHAY buh-ZWAH duh ruh-noo-vuh-LAY mohn ohr-doh-NAHNS.

I'm allergic to [medication/food] and need to avoid it.
Je suis allergique à [médicament/nourriture] et j'ai besoin de l'éviter.
ZHuh swee zhal-ur-ZHEEK ah [may-dee-kuh-MAWN/noo-ree-TYUR] ay zhay buh-ZWAH duh lay-vee-TAY.

I've been feeling tired and rundown lately.
Je me sens fatigué(e) et épuisé(e) dernièrement.
ZHuh muh sahns fah-tee-GAY(e) ay ay-pwee-ZAY dern-YAY-mahn.

I need to discuss my test results with the doctor.
J'ai besoin de discuter de mes résultats de test avec le médecin.
ZHAY buh-ZWAH duh dee-skoo-TAY duh may ray-zool-TAH duh tayst ay-ek luh MAY-duh-sahn.

I'm having trouble sleeping.
J'ai des problèmes de sommeil.
ZHAY day proh-BLEM duh sohm-MAY.

I need a flu shot or other vaccine.
J'ai besoin d'un vaccin contre la grippe ou autre.
ZHAY buh-ZWAH duhn vak-AN kohntr luh grihp oo oh-truh.

I'm pregnant and need to discuss my prenatal care.
Je suis enceinte et j'ai besoin de discuter de mes soins prénatals.
ZHuh swee zahn-SAYNT ay zhay buh-ZWAH duh dee-skoo-TAY duh may swahn pray-nah-TAHL.

I've been experiencing some side effects from my medication.
J'ai eu des effets secondaires de mon médicament.
ZHAY uh day zay-FAY suh-gon-DAIR duh mohn may-dee-kuh-MAWN.

I need a physical exam.
J'ai besoin d'un examen physique.
ZHAY buh-ZWAH duhn egz-ah-MAN fih-zik.

I need a note for work or school.
J'ai besoin d'une note pour le travail ou l'école.
ZHAY buh-ZWAH duhn noht poor luh truh-VYAH oh leh-KOHL.

I need to discuss my diet and nutrition with the doctor.
J'ai besoin de discuter de mon régime alimentaire et de ma nutrition avec le médecin.
ZHAY buh-ZWAH duh dee-skoo-TEH duh mohn ray-ZHEEM
ahl-mahn-TEHR ay duh mah new-tree-SYOHN avek luh may-duh-SAHN.

I need to have my blood pressure checked.
Je dois faire vérifier ma tension artérielle.
ZHuh dwah fair veh-ree-FYAY mah tahn-see-YOHN ar-teh-ree-YELL.

I have a cough or sore throat.
J'ai une toux ou mal à la gorge.
ZHAY ewn too oo mahl ah la gawrzh.

I have a fever or other flu-like symptoms.
J'ai de la fièvre ou d'autres symptômes semblables à la grippe.
ZHAY duh lah fee-EHVRE oo dohtr sohm-bleh ah lah grip.

I need a prescription for a medication.
J'ai besoin d'une ordonnance pour un médicament.
ZHAY buh-ZWAH duhn or-doh-NAHNS poor uh may-dee-ka-MAHN.

I have an appointment with the doctor.
J'ai un rendez-vous avec le médecin.
ZHAY uh ran-day-voo avek luh may-duh-SAHN.

AT THE DENTIST

I have an appointment with Dr. _____.
J'ai un rendez-vous avec le Docteur _____.
Zhay uh RON-day-voo a-vek luh dok-TUHR

I'm here for my dental checkup.
Je suis ici pour ma visite dentaire.
Zhuh swee e-see poor ma vee-ZEET duhn-TEHR

I need to schedule a cleaning.
J'ai besoin de prendre rendez-vous pour un nettoyage.
Zhay buh-ZWAHN duh prahn-druh RON-day-voo poor uhn nuh-twah-YAHZH

I have a toothache.
J'ai mal aux dents.
Zhay mal oh dahn

I'm experiencing sensitivity in my teeth.
J'ai de la sensibilité dentaire.
Zhay duh lah sahn-see-bee-lee-tay duhn-TEHR

I broke a tooth and need it repaired.
Je me suis cassé une dent et j'ai besoin de la faire réparer.
Zhuh muh swee kah-SAY uhn dahn ay zhay buh-ZWAHN duh lah fair ruh-pah-RAY

I lost a filling and need it replaced.
J'ai perdu un plombage et j'ai besoin de le faire remplacer.
Zhay pair-doo uh plom-BAZH ay zhay buh-ZWAHN duh luh fair rahm-pluh-SAY

I have a cavity that needs to be filled.
J'ai une carie qui doit être soignée.
ZHAY oon kah-REE keuh dwa etruh swa-NAY

I need a dental X-ray.
J'ai besoin d'une radiographie dentaire.
ZHAY buh-ZWAH duhn RAH-dee-oh-graf-ee dahn-TEHR

I'm interested in teeth whitening.
Je suis intéressé(e) par le blanchiment des dents.
Zhuh swee-zaN-tay-reh-say pahr luh blahn-sheuh-mahn day dahn

Can you recommend a good toothpaste?
Pouvez-vous recommander une bonne pâte dentifrice ?
Poo-veh voo ruh-koh-mahn-DAY ewn bawn paht den-tee-free-suh

How often should I floss?
À quelle fréquence devrais-je utiliser le fil dentaire ?
Ah kell freh-kahns duh-vrehzh zhuh oo-tee-lee-zay luh feel dahn-tair

Do you have any tips for improving my dental hygiene?
Avez-vous des conseils pour améliorer mon hygiène dentaire?
Ah-veh voo day kohn-seel poor ah-may-lee-oh-reh mohn eezh-yehn dahn-tair

How long will the procedure take?
Combien de temps durera la procédure?
Kohm-BYAN duh tahN doo-REH-rah lah proh-say-DOOR

Will I need any anesthesia?
Est-ce que j'aurai besoin d'une anesthésie?
Ess-kuh zho-REH buh-ZWAH duhn ah-nes-teh-ZEE

How much will the procedure cost?
Combien coûtera la procédure ?
Kohm-BYAN koo-TUH-ruh lah proh-SAY-dur?

Do you accept insurance?
Acceptez-vous l'assurance ?
Ahk-sep-teh voo lah-suh-RAHNS?

Can you explain the procedure to me?
Pouvez-vous m'expliquer la procédure ?
Poo-vay voo meks-plee-KAY lah proh-SAY-dur?

Is there any discomfort associated with the procedure?
Y a-t-il un malaise associé à la procédure ?
Ee ah-TEEL uhn mah-LEZ ah-soh-see-AY ah lah proh-SAY-dur?

How long will it take for me to recover?
Combien de temps vais-je prendre pour récupérer ?
Kohm-BYAN duh tahN vayzh prahn-druh poor ree-koo-peh-ray?

Can I eat or drink anything before the procedure?
Puis-je manger ou boire quelque chose avant la procédure ?
pweeZH mahN-zhay oo bwahr kuhl-kuh SHOZ ah-vahn lah proh-SAY-dur?

Will I need someone to drive me home after the procedure?
Ai-je besoin de quelqu'un pour me conduire à la maison après la procédure ?
Ay zhuh buh-ZWAHN duh kuhl-kuh pohr muh kohN-dweer ah lah meh-ZOHn ah-PREH lah proh-SAY-dur?

Will I need to take any medication after the procedure?
Devrai-je prendre des médicaments après la procédure ?
Duh-vray zhuh prahN-druh day may-dee-kuh-MAHN ah-preh lah proh-SAY-dur?

Can you give me a prescription for pain medication?
Pouvez-vous me donner une ordonnance pour des médicaments contre la douleur ?
Poo-veh-VOO muh doh-NAY une or-doh-NAHSS poor dey med-ee-kah-mahnts kohn-truh la doo-LEUR?

How often should I come in for a checkup?
À quelle fréquence devrais-je venir pour un contrôle ?
Ah KELL freh-KAHNS duh-vrehzh zhuh vuh-NEER poor uhn kohn-TROHL?

Can you recommend any oral hygiene products?
Pouvez-vous recommander des produits d'hygiène bucco-dentaire ?
Poo-veh-VOO ruh-koh-mahn-DAY dey proh-dwee d'ee-zhee-EN buh-koh-duhn-TAIR?

Can you show me how to properly brush and floss my teeth?
Pouvez-vous me montrer comment bien brosser et passer la soie dentaire?
Poo-veh-VOO muh mohn-TRAY koh-mohn byen bro-SAY ay pah-SAY lah SWAH duhn-TAIR?

Do you have any aftercare instructions for me?
Avez-vous des instructions de soins après traitement pour moi?
Ah-veh-VOO deez een-struhk-see-ohn duh SWAHN ah-pray trah-tuh-MAHN poor mwah?

Can you schedule my next appointment?
Pouvez-vous planifier mon prochain rendez-vous?
Poo-veh-VOO plah-nee-FYAY mohn proh-SHEN ron-day-VOO?

Thank you, see you next time.
Merci, à la prochaine.
Mehr-SEE, ah lah proh-SHEN.

COMMON QUESTIONS WHEN ENTERING A NEW COUNTRY

What is the currency used in this country?
Quelle est la monnaie utilisée dans ce pays ?
KELL eh lah moh-NAY ew-til-ih-ZEH dahn suh PAYS ?

Where can I exchange my money?
Où puis-je changer de l'argent ?
OO pwis-JUH shahn-ZHEH duh LAHN-zhah?

What is the local language?
Quelle est la langue locale ?
KELL eh lah LAHNG luh-KAHL ?

Do people here speak English?
Est-ce que les gens parlent anglais ici ?
ESS-kuh lay zhan PAHR-leh ahn-GLAY ee-see?

How do I get to my accommodation?
Comment puis-je me rendre à mon logement ?
KOH-mahn pwis-JUH muh RON-druh ah mohn lohzh-MAHN?

Is public transportation reliable?
Est-ce que les transports en commun sont fiables ?
ESS-kuh lay trahn-SPOR-tahn kaw-MUHN sohn fee-AH-bluh?

How do I buy a public transportation ticket?
Comment acheter un billet de transport en commun ?
KOH-mahn toh-SHAY uhn bee-YAY duh trahn-SPOR-tahn kaw-MUHN ?

Are there any cultural norms I should be aware of?
Y a-t-il des normes culturelles dont je devrais être conscient ?
EE-aht-eel day NOR-muh kool-TU-rel dohn zhuh duh-vreh eht-tuh kohn-see-AHN?

What are the emergency phone numbers?
Quels sont les numéros d'urgence ?
KELL-sohn lay noo-MEH-roh dur-ZHONSS?

Are there any dangerous areas I should avoid?
Y a-t-il des zones dangereuses à éviter ?
EE-aht-eel day ZOHN don-zhehr uh EV-ee-tay?

What are the local foods and drinks?
Quels sont les plats et boissons locaux ?
KELL-sohn lay plah ay bwa-SOHNS loh-KOH?

How do I order food in a restaurant?
Comment commander de la nourriture dans un restaurant ?
KOH-mahn koh-mahn-DAYR duh lah noo-ree-TOOR dahn uhn rah-stoh-RAHN?

Can I drink tap water here?
Puis-je boire l'eau du robinet ici ?
POO-ee zhuh bwa-RUH loh DOO roh-beh-NAY ee-see?

What are the electricity voltage and plugs used here?
Quelle est la tension électrique et les prises utilisées ici ?
KELL eh lah TAHN-see-ohn ay-LEK-treek ay lay PREEZ ew-til-ih-ZEH ee-see?

Is it safe to use public Wi-Fi?
Est-ce sûr d'utiliser le Wi-Fi public ?
ESS-kuh syoor doh-tee-lee-zay luh WEE-fee puh-BLEEK?

How do I get a local SIM card?
Comment obtenir une carte SIM locale ?
KOH-mahn oh-btuh-NEER ewn kahrt SIM loh-KAHL?

What are the popular tourist attractions?
Quelles sont les attractions touristiques populaires ?
KELL-sohn lay aht-trahk-see-YOHNS too-ree-STEEK pop-yuh-LAIR?

What is the weather like here?
Comment est le temps ici ?
KOH-mahn eh luh TAHMP ee-see?

What are the best ways to stay safe?
Quelles sont les meilleures façons de rester en sécurité ?
KELL-sohn lay may-yuhr FAH-sohn duh ruh-STAY ahn seh-kew-REE-tay?

How do I get medical help if I need it?
Comment obtenir de l'aide médicale si j'en ai besoin ?
KOH-mahn oh-btuh-NEER duh leed may-dee-KAHL see zhahn eh NAY buh-ZWAHN?

Are there any laws or regulations I should be aware of?
Y a-t-il des lois ou des règlements dont je devrais être conscient ?
EE-aht-eel day loh oo day ray-gluh-MAHNG dohn zhuh duh-vreh eh-truh kohN-see-AHN?

How do I use public restrooms?
Comment utiliser les toilettes publiques ?
KOH-mahn-t ew-tee-lee-ZAY lay twa-LETT puh-BLEEK?

What are the local shopping hours?
Quelles sont les heures d'ouverture des magasins locaux ?
KELL-sohn lay EUHR doo-VEHR-tewr day mah-gah-SAHN loh-KOH?

How do I make phone calls from here?
Comment passer des appels téléphoniques d'ici ?
KOH-mahn pah-SAY day za-PEL tay-lay-FOH-NEEK dee-see?

How do I connect to the internet?
Comment me connecter à internet ?
KOH-mahn muh koh-NEK-tay ah ahN-tuhr-NET?

Are there any local holidays or festivals coming up?
Y a-t-il des fêtes ou des jours fériés locaux à venir ?
EE ah-TEEL day FET oh day JUHR FAY-ree-ay loh-KOH ah vuh-NIHR ?

How do I navigate the local transportation system?
Comment puis-je naviguer dans le système de transport local ?
KOH-mohn PWEEZH nah-vee-guh day loh-SIS-tuhm duh trahn-SPOHR loh-KAHL ?

Are there any local SIM cards that offer data plans for my phone?
Y a-t-il des cartes SIM locales qui offrent des forfaits de données pour mon téléphone ?
EE ah-TEEL day KART SIM loh-KAHL kuh oh-FRAY day fohr-FAY duh dah-TAH pohr mohn tay-lay-FOHN ?

What is the local cuisine like and what are some must-try dishes?
Comment est la cuisine locale et quels sont les plats incontournables ?
KOH-mohn ay lah kwee-ZEEN loh-KAHL ay kell sohn lay PLAH ahn-kohn-too-RAHBL ?

What are the typical hours of operation for shops, restaurants, and attractions?
Quelles sont les heures d'ouverture typiques des magasins, restaurants et attractions ?
KELL sohn lay EUR duh-vair-TOOR tee-PEEK day mah-GAH-sahn, rah-stoh-RAHN, ay ah-trahk-SEE-OHN ?

How do I purchase tickets for tourist attractions or events?
Comment acheter des billets pour les attractions touristiques ou les événements ?
KOH-mohn oh-SHAY day bee-YAY pour lay ah-trahk-SEE-OHN too-ris-TEEK oh lay ay-vay-NAY-mohn ?

What is the local dress code?
Quel est le code vestimentaire local ?
KELL ay luh KOHD ve-stee-mahn-TAIR loh-KAHL ?

What are the local customs and attitudes towards bargaining and haggling?
Quelles sont les coutumes locales et les attitudes en matière de marchandage et de négociation ?
KELL sohn lay koo-TOOM loh-KAHL ay lay ah-tee-TYUD on mah-TEER duh mar-shahn-DAHZH ay duh nay-goh-see-ah-SYON ?

How do I obtain a visa extension if needed?
Comment puis-je obtenir une extension de visa si nécessaire ?
KOH-mohn PWEEZH zho-buh-TEH-nir yoon ek-stahn-SYON duh vee-ZAH see nay-say-SAYR ?

What are some popular local phrases or slang that I should be familiar with?

Quelles sont les phrases ou expressions locales populaires que je devrais connaître ?

KELL sohn lay frahz oh ayks-pray-SYON loh-KAHL pop-yuh-LAIR kuh zhuh duh-vreh coh-nay-TR ?

She's kind and helpful.
Elle est gentille et serviable.
EL-uh eh zhahn-TEEY euh sehr-vee-ah-bluh.

He's smart and hardworking.
Il est intelligent et travailleur.
EEL eh-tahn-lee-zhahng eh trah-vah-YUHR.

She's creative and talented.
Elle est créative et talentueuse.
EL-uh eh krey-AH-tee-vuh ey tal-ahn-TEUHZ.

He's confident and charismatic.
Il est confiant et charismatique.
EEL eh kawn-FYAHNG ey shah-reez-mah-TEEK.

She's reliable and responsible.
Elle est fiable et responsable.
EL-uh eh fee-AHBL ey reh-spohn-SAHBL.

Confident.
Confiant/e.
Kawn-FYAHNG.

Cautious.
Prudent/e.
Proo-DAHNG.

Brave.
Brave/e.
BRAHV.

Fearful.
Craintif/Craintive.
KRAWN-teef/KRAWN-teev.

Careless.
Négligent/e.
NAY-glee-zhahn/ NAY-glee-zhahnt.

Meticulous.
Méticuleux/Méticuleuse.
May-tee-kew-LUH/May-tee-kew-LUHZ.

Energetic.
Énergique.
EY-nair-zheeK.

Laid-back.
Détendu/e.
Day-tahn-doo.

Creative.
Créatif/Créative.
Krey-AH-teeF/Krey-AH-teeV.

Logical.
Logique.
Loh-geek.

Ambitious.
Ambitieux/Ambitieuse.
AHM-bee-tyuh/AHM-bee-tyuhz.

Humble.
Modeste.
Moh-DEST.

Arrogant.
Arrogant/e.
AH-roh-GAHNG.

Thoughtful.
Réfléchi/e.
Ray-flay-SHEE.

Impulsive
Impulsif
Ihm-pul-SEEF

Patient
Patient
Pah-see-ahn

Impatient
Impatient
Ihm-pah-see-ahn

Sociable
Sociable
Soh-see-ah-bluh

Reserved
Réservé(e)
Reh-zehr-VAY

Reliable
Fiable
Fee-ah-bluh

Unreliable
Peu fiable
Puh fee-ah-bluh

Diligent
Diligent(e)
Dee-lee-zhahn

Lazy
Paresseux/paresseuse
Pahr-eh-suh/pahr-eh-suhz

Outgoing
Extraverti(e)
Ehks-trah-VEHR-tee

Introverted
Introverti(e)
Ahn-troh-VEHR-tee

Impressive
Impressionnant(e)
Ihm-preh-syoh-NAHN/ihm-preh-syoh-NAHNT

Mediocre
Médiocre
Meh-dee-oh-kr

Enthusiastic
Enthousiaste
Ehn-too-zee-ahst

Lackadaisical
Nonchalant(e)
Nohn-shah-lahn/ nohn-shah-lahn-tuh

Punctual
Ponctuel(le)
Pohnk-tuh-EL/ pohnk-tuh-ELL

The view is beautiful.
La vue est magnifique.
LAH vew eh mah-NI-fee-k.

The decor is stylish.
La décoration est élégante.
LAH day-koh-ra-see-YOHNG eh ay-LEH-gahnt.

The food is delicious.
La nourriture est délicieuse.
LAH noo-ree-TUHR eh day-lee-see-YUZ.

The room is cozy.
La chambre est confortable.
LAH sham-bruh eh kohn-for-TAHBL.

The car is luxurious.
La voiture est luxueuse.
LAH vwah-tyoor eh luks-YUZ.

TALKING ABOUT HOBBIES AND INTERESTS

I love reading books.
Je suis passionnée de lecture.
Zhuh swee pah-see-oh-NEY duh lek-TYUR

Cooking is my favorite hobby.
La cuisine est mon passe-temps préféré.
La kwee-ZEHN eh mohn pahs-uh-TEMPS pray-fuh-RAY

I enjoy playing video games.
J'aime jouer aux jeux vidéo.
Zhem joo-AY oh zheuh VEH-dee-oh

Painting is a great way to relax.
La peinture est un excellent moyen de se détendre.
La pehn-TUHR eh uhn ehks-eh-LAHN mwehN duh suh deh-TAHND-ruh

Watching movies is my go-to activity.
Regarder des films est mon activité favorite.
Ruh-gar-DAY deh feel eh mohn ak-tee-VEE-tay fah-voh-REE-tuh

I love to travel and explore new places.
J'adore voyager et découvrir de nouveaux endroits.
Zhah-DOR vwa-ya-ZHAY ay day-koo-VREER duh noo-VOH-ZON-dro

I'm passionate about photography.
Je suis passionnée de photographie.
Zhuh swee pah-see-oh-NEY duh foh-toh-GRAH-fee

Music is my escape from reality.
La musique est mon échappatoire de la réalité.
La mew-ZEEK eh mohn ay-shap-ah-TWAHR duh lah reh-ah-lee-TAY

Gardening is my way of connecting with nature.
Le jardinage est ma façon de me connecter avec la nature.
*Luh jahr-dee-NAZH eh mah fah-SAWN duh muh kohn-NEK-teh a-vehk
lah nah-TYUR*

I enjoy hiking and being outdoors.
J'aime faire de la randonnée et être en plein air.
Zhem fayr duh lah rahn-doh-NAY ay etruh ahN plehN EHHR

Dancing is my favorite way to exercise.
La danse est ma façon préférée de faire de l'exercice.
La dahns eh mah fah-SAWN pray-fay-RAY duh fair duh leks-ehr-SEES

I love to write short stories and poems.
J'adore écrire des histoires courtes et des poèmes.
Zhah-DOR ay-KREE-ruh dayz ee-STWAHR koorT ay day poh-EM

Playing sports is my favorite way to stay active.
Jouer à des sports est ma façon préférée de rester actifve.
Zhoo-AY ah day spor eh mah fah-SAWN pray-fay-RAY duh ruh-STAY ahk-TEEF

I'm an avid collector of stamps and coins.
Je suis une collectionneureuse passionnée de timbres et de pièces de monnaie.
Zhuh swee uhn koh-lek-see-YOH-ruh pah-see-oh-NEY duh tahn-bruh ay duh pyehs duh moh-NAY

I enjoy knitting and crocheting.
J'aime tricoter et crocheter.
Zhuh EM tree-ko-TAY ay kroh-SHAY-tay

I love to go fishing in my free time.
J'adore pêcher pendant mon temps libre.
Zhah-DOR peh-SHAY pahn-dohn mohn tahn lee-bruh

Learning new languages is a hobby of mine.
Apprendre de nouvelles langues est mon hobby.
Ah-prahN-druh duh noo-VEL lahng eh mohn OH-bee

I enjoy playing board games with friends.
J'aime jouer à des jeux de société avec des amis.
Zhuh EM joo-AY ah day zheuh duh soh-see-eh-tay ah-vehk dayz ah-MEE

Yoga and meditation help me relax and de-stress.
Le yoga et la méditation m'aident à me détendre et à réduire le stress.
Luh yoh-GAH eh lah may-dee-ta-see-YOH mah-ee-dawn-tay ah muh
day-TAHND-ruh ay ah reh-dweer luh stress

I'm passionate about baking and pastry making.
Je suis passionnée de pâtisserie et de boulangerie.
Zhuh swee pah-see-oh-NEY duh pah-tees-REE ay duh
boo-lawn-ZHEH-ree

Watching and playing sports is my favorite pastime.
Regarder et jouer des sports est mon passe-temps préféré.
Ruh-gar-DAY ay joo-AY day spor eh mohn pahs-TOHNG pray-fay-RAY

I love to go camping and hiking in the mountains.
J'aime aller camper et faire de la randonnée en montagne.
Zhuh EM ah-lay kahm-PAY ay fayr duh lah rahn-doh-NAY ahn
mohn-TAHN-yuh

Reading and writing about history is my passion.
Lire et écrire sur l'histoire est ma passion.
LEER ay ay-KREE-ruh sir lees-TWAHR eh mah pah-see-YOHNG

I'm an amateur astronomer and love stargazing.
Je suis une astronome amateure et j'aime observer les étoiles.
Zhuh swee uhn as-truh-NOHM ah-muh-TUHR ay zhuh-EM ohb-sair-vay
layz ay-TWAHL

I enjoy watching and collecting classic movies.
J'aime regarder et collectionner des films classiques.
Zhuh EM ruh-gar-DAY ay koh-lek-see-YOH-ner day feelm klah-SEEK

Playing musical instruments is my hobby.
Jouer d'instruments de musique est mon passe-temps.
Joo-AY dahn-stroo-mahn duh moo-ZEEK eh mohn pahs-TOHNG

I love to cook and experiment with new recipes.
J'adore cuisiner et expérimenter de nouvelles recettes.
Zhah-DOR kwee-zi-NAY ay ehk-spair-ee-mahn-TAY duh noo-VEL ruh-SEHT

I enjoy going to the gym and working out.
J'aime aller à la salle de gym et faire de l'exercice.
Zhuh EM ah-lay ah lah sal duh zhimm ay fayr duh leks-ehr-SEES

I love to knit and make scarves and hats.
J'adore tricoter et faire des écharpes et des chapeaux.
Zhah-DOR tree-ko-TAY ay fayr dayz eh-SKAR-puh ay day shap-oh

Painting and drawing are my favorite ways to express myself.
La peinture et le dessin sont mes façons préférées de m'exprimer.
Lah pan-TUHR ay luh deh-SAN son meh fah-SAWN pray-fay-RAY duh mehks-pruh-MAY

Let's meet up.
Retrouvons-nous.
Ruh-TROO-von noo.

How about we grab lunch?
Et si on déjeunait ensemble ?
EH see ohn deh-JUH-nay ahn-SAHM-bluh.

Do you want to hang out?
Tu veux passer du temps ensemble ?
TUH veuh pass-AY dueh tahnSAHM-bluh.

I was thinking we could go to the movies.
Je pensais qu'on pourrait aller au cinéma.
Juh pahn-SAY kuh puh-RAH al-AYR sih-NAY-ma.

Want to go for a walk?
On va se promener ?
Ohn vah suh proh-muh-NAY.

Let's have dinner together.
Dînons ensemble.
Dee-NOHnS ahn-SAHM-bluh.

We should go out and do something.
On devrait sortir et faire quelque chose.
Ohn duh-vreh sohr-TEER ay fair kel-kuh CHOHZ.

How about we go shopping?
Et si on faisait du shopping ?
EH see ohn fay-ZAY dew SHOP-PEENG.

Let's have a picnic.
Faisons un pique-nique.
Fay-ZOHnS uhn peek-NEEK.

We should plan a trip.
On devrait planifier un voyage.
Ohn duh-vreh plah-nee-FEE-ay uhn vwa-YAHZH.

Want to go to a concert?
Tu veux aller à un concert ?
TUH veuh zah-LAYR ahn un kon-SAIR.

Let's catch up over coffee.
Retrouvons-nous autour d'un café.
Ruh-TROO-von noo oh-TOUR dun kah-FAY.

How about we go to the beach?
Et si on allait à la plage ?
EH see ohn ah-LAY ah lah PLAHZH.

We should check out that new restaurant.
On devrait aller voir ce nouveau restaurant.
Ohn duh-vreh ah-LAYR vwahrs suh noo-VOH rah-stoh-RAHN.

Let's have a game night.
Organisons une soirée jeux.
Ohr-gah-nee-SONZ uhn SWAH-ray juh.

How about a bike ride?
Et si on faisait du vélo ?
EH see ohn fay-ZAY dew VAY-loh.

Want to go for a hike?
Tu veux aller faire une randonnée ?
TUH veuh zah-LAYR fair ewn rahn-doh-NAY.

We should go to the museum.
On devrait aller au musée.
Ohn duh-vreh ah-LAYR oh mew-ZAY.

Let's go to the park.
Allons au parc.
AH-lohn oh pahrk.

How about a day trip?
Et si on faisait une excursion d'une journée ?
EH see ohn fay-ZAY ewn ehks-kooz-ee-ohn dewn johr-NAY.

We should go to the gym together.
On devrait aller au gym ensemble.
Ohn duh-vreh ah-LAYR oh zhimm ahn-SAHM-bluh.

Want to go to the zoo?
Tu veux aller au zoo ?
TUH veuh zah-LAYR oh zoo.

Let's go to the farmers market.
Allons au marché fermier.
AH-lohn oh mar-SHAY fer-MYAY.

How about we go to a comedy show?
Et si on allait à un spectacle comique ?
EH see ohn ah-LAY ahn un spek-TAH-kluh-koom-EK.

We should have a barbecue.
On devrait faire un barbecue.
Ohn duh-vreh fair uhn bar-bih-KYOO.

Want to go to the art gallery?
Tu veux aller à la galerie d'art ?
TUH veuh zah-LAYR ah lah ga-luh-REE dar.

Let's go to a sporting event.
Allons à un événement sportif.
AH-lohn ahn ew-VEH-nuh-mahn spohr-TEE.

We should go to the theater.
On devrait aller au théâtre.
Ohn duh-vreh ah-LAYR oh tay-AH-truh.

How about a weekend getaway?
Et si on faisait une escapade de fin de semaine ?
EH see ohn fay-ZAY ewn es-kah-PAHD duh fahn duh se-MEHN.

Let's plan a birthday party.

Organisons une fête d'anniversaire.

Ohr-gah-nee-SONZ ewn fet dan-ee-vair-SAIR

What time do you wake up?
À quelle heure vous réveillez-vous?
AH kelle uhr voo ray-vay-EE voo?

Do you have a morning routine?
Avez-vous une routine matinale?
AH-vay voo oon roo-TEEN ma-tee-NAHL?

Do you exercise daily?
Faites-vous de l'exercice tous les jours?
FET voo duh LEKS-er-SEH too ley ZHOOR?

What time do you go to bed?
À quelle heure allez-vous au lit?
AH kelle uhr ah-lay-VOO oh lee?

What's your favorite part of your daily routine?
Quelle est votre partie préférée de votre routine quotidienne?
KELL eh voh-truh pahr-TEE pray-fair-AY duh voh-truh roo-TEEN kwo-ti-DYEN?

Do you have any daily hobbies or activities
Avez-vous des passe-temps ou des activités quotidiennes?
AH-vay voo day pahs-TEM oo day-za-ktee-VEE ko-ti-DYEN?

Would you like to change anything about your daily routine?
Voudriez-vous changer quelque chose dans votre routine quotidienne?
Voo-dree-AY-voo shahn-ZHAY kel-kuh SHOZ dan voh-truh roo-TEEN kwo-ti-DYEN?

I commute to work/school.
Je fais la navette pour aller travailler / à l'école.
Zhuh fet lah na-VET poor ah-lay trav-eye-YAY / ah lay-SKOLE.

I take a walk during my lunch break.
Je fais une promenade pendant ma pause déjeuner.
Zhuh fet oon pro-muh-nad pahn-dahn ma pohz day-zheu-NAY.

I continue working/studying in the afternoon.
Je continue à travailler/étudier l'après-midi.
Zhuh kohn-tee-NOO ah trah-vah-YAY/eh-too-dyay lah-preh-mee-DEE.

I have a snack in the afternoon.
Je prends une collation l'après-midi.
Zhuh prohnz oon koh-lah-syon lah-preh-mee-DEE.

I commute back home.
Je fais la navette pour rentrer chez moi.
Zhuh fay lah nah-VEHT poor ran-TRAY shay mwah.

I read a book in the evening.
Je lis un livre le soir.
Zhuh leez un liv-ruh luh swah.

I take a bath or shower before bed.
Je prends un bain ou une douche avant d'aller me coucher.
Zhuh prahn un ban oo oon doosh ah-vahn dal-ay may koo-shay.

I brush my teeth before bed.
Je me brosse les dents avant d'aller au lit.
Zhuh muh bross lay dahn ah-vahn dal-ay oh lee.

I go to bed at...
Je vais au lit à...
Zhuh vay oh lee tah...

I fall asleep quickly.
Je m'endors rapidement.
Zhuh mahn-dor rap-ee-doh-mahn.

I wake up in the middle of the night.
Je me réveille au milieu de la nuit.
Zhuh muh ray-vay-ye oh mee-lee-eu duh lah nwee.

I have trouble falling back to sleep.

J'ai du mal à me rendormir.

Zhay doo mahl ah muh rahn-dor-meer.

You should take a break and relax for a while.
Vous devriez prendre une pause et vous détendre pendant un moment.
VOO dev-REE prahn-druhn pohz ay voo day-TAHN-dr pahn-dahn uhn moh-MON.

I think it would be a good idea to talk to someone about this.
Je pense que ce serait une bonne idée d'en parler à quelqu'un.
ZUH PANS kuh suh-SRAY uhn BOHN-nee day DAWN parl-AY ah kel-KUN.

If I were you, I would consider taking a different approach.
Si j'étais à votre place, je songerais à adopter une approche différente.
Sh ZHE-tay ah vohtr plahs, zhuh song-er-AY ah ah-dop-TAY uhn ah-PROSH dee-FEH-rahn-tuh.

You might want to try looking at the problem from a different perspective.
Vous pourriez essayer de regarder le problème d'un autre point de vue.
VOO poor-REE ess-AY-ee duh ruh-gar-DAY luh proh-BLEM dahn O-nuh-tr pwahn duh vu.

It could be helpful to make a list of pros and cons before making a decision.
Il pourrait être utile de dresser une liste des avantages et des inconvénients avant de prendre une décision.
El poor-RAH-ee eh-tuh ew-TEEL duh dress-AY uhn leest dayz ah-vahn-TAZH ey dayz an-kon-VAY-nyahn ah-vahn duh pruh-NDR uh day-si-ZYON.

Have you considered seeking professional help?
Avez-vous envisagé de demander de l'aide professionnelle ?
AHvay-VOO ahn-vee-ZAH-zhay duh dahn-MAN-day duh lah-EED proh-fess-ee-oh-NELL.

You should prioritize your tasks and focus on the most important ones first.

Vous devriez donner la priorité à vos tâches et vous concentrer sur les plus importantes en premier.

VOO dev-REE doh-NAY lah pree-oh-REE-tay ah voh task ey voo kon-sahn-TRAY sir lay ploo-zahn-POR-tahnt ah pruh-MYAY.

It might be a good idea to take a step back and think things through.

Il pourrait être judicieux de prendre du recul et de réfléchir.

Eel poor-RAH-ee eh-tuh zhew-dee-SYUH duh prahn-druh dew ruh-KOOL ey duh ray-flay-SHEER.

You need to be more assertive and stand up for yourself.

Vous devez être plus assertif et vous affirmer.

VOO duh-VAYT etr pluhs ah-sair-TEEf ey voo ah-fee-MAY.

Don't be afraid to ask for help when you need it.

N'ayez pas peur de demander de l'aide lorsque vous en avez besoin.

Neh-yay pah pur duh-mahn-day duh lah-EED lor-SKuh voo zahn-AYZ buh-SOHN.

It might be beneficial to do some research before making a decision.

Il pourrait être bénéfique de faire des recherches avant de prendre une décision.

Eel poor-RAH-ee eh-tuh bey-nay-fee-EEK duh fair day ruh-SHAYRCH avahn duh pruhndr uh day-si-ZYON.

You should try to see the situation from the other person's point of view.

Vous devriez essayer de voir la situation du point de vue de l'autre personne.

VOO dev-REE ess-AY-ee duh vwahr lah see-too-ah-SYON doo pwahn duh vu duh lo-truh pur-SON.

I suggest you set realistic goals that are achievable.

Je vous suggère de fixer des objectifs réalistes qui sont atteignables.

Zhuh voo suh-ZHEHR duh feek-SAY dayz ob-jek-TEEF reh-ah-LEEST kee son ah-tey-NYAHBL.

It's important to take care of yourself both physically and mentally.
Il est important de prendre soin de soi-même tant physiquement que mentalement.
Eel eh-tah pore-tahn duh prahndr swahn duh swah-mem tohn fee-zee-kemahn keuh mahn-tahl-mahn.

You should try to communicate your feelings more effectively.
Vous devriez essayer de communiquer vos sentiments de manière plus efficace.
VOO dev-REE ess-AY-ee duh koh-mewn-ee-KAY voh sahN-tee-mohn duh mahn-YAIR pluhs eh-fee-KASS.

What do you think I should do in this situation?
Qu'est-ce que vous pensez que je devrais faire dans cette situation ?
Kest-kuh voo PAHN-say kuh zhuh duh-vreh fair dahn sEt swah-tee-ah-SYON.

Can you give me some advice on how to handle this?
Pouvez-vous me donner des conseils sur la façon de gérer cela ?
Poo-VAY voo muh doh-nay day kawn-seal sur lah fah-SAWN duh zhey-ray suh-lah.

What would you do if you were in my shoes?
Que feriez-vous si vous étiez à ma place ?
Kuh feh-ree-AY voo sih voo EH-tee-ay ah mah plahs.

I'm not sure what to do, can you help me?
Je ne suis pas sûr de ce que je dois faire, pouvez-vous m'aider ?
Zhuh nuh swee pah sur duh suh kuh zhuh doo fair, puh-vay voo may-day.

Do you have any suggestions on how to approach this problem?
Avez-vous des suggestions sur la façon d'aborder ce problème ?
Ah-vay voo day suh-jes-TYON sur lah fah-SAWN dah-bor-DAY suh proh-BLEM.

How can I improve my situation?
Comment puis-je améliorer ma situation ?
KOH-mah PWEED j'AMAY-LEE-OH-rer ma see-too-AH-syohn ?

What steps can I take to resolve this issue?
Quelles sont les étapes que je peux prendre pour résoudre ce problème ?
KELL sohn lay-TAP keuh zhuh puh PRAHND-ra pour ray-ZOHL-druh suh PRO-blem ?

Can you offer any guidance on how to deal with this?
Pouvez-vous offrir des conseils sur la façon de traiter cela ?
Poo-vay VOOZ oh-freer day kohn-SAYL sur la fah-SAWN duh TRAY-tay suh-lah ?

I'm feeling lost, do you have any advice on how to find my way?
Je me sens perdue, avez-vous des conseils sur la façon de trouver mon chemin ?
Zhuh muh sahn pehr-dew, ah-vay-VOO day kohn-SAYL sur la fah-SAWN duh troo-vay mawn sheh-MEHN ?

What are your thoughts on how to move forward?
Quelles sont vos réflexions sur la façon d'avancer ?
KELL sohn voh ray-FLEK-syon sur la fah-SAWN davawn-SAY ?

What advice would you give me to help me succeed?
Quels conseils me donneriez-vous pour m'aider à réussir ?
KELL kohn-SAYL muh doh-nuh-ree-ay VOO pour may-DAY ah ray-OO-SEER ?

How can I overcome this obstacle?
Comment puis-je surmonter cet obstacle ?
KOH-mah PWEEZH suhr-mawn-TAY set ohbstah-kleuh ?

Can you recommend any resources that might be helpful?
Pouvez-vous recommander des ressources qui pourraient être utiles ?
Poo-vay VOO ruh-koh-man-day day ruh-SAWRS kee poor-RAH-ee ayt-EE?

I need some direction, can you point me in the right direction?
J'ai besoin de direction, pouvez-vous m'indiquer la bonne voie ?
Zhay buh-ZWAHN duh dir-ehk-syon, poo-vay VOO mawn-dee-KAY la bohn VWAH ?

What strategies would you suggest to help me achieve my goals?
Quelles stratégies suggéreriez-vous pour m'aider à atteindre mes objectifs ?
KELL strat-AY-zhee suh-zjeh-RYE-ree-ay VOO pour may-DAY ah-tendr muh-zohbj-ehk-teef ?

TALKING ABOUT LIKES AND DISLIKES

I love chocolate.
J'adore le chocolat.
ZHAD-OR luh shoh-koh-LAH

I really enjoy listening to music.
J'aime beaucoup écouter de la musique.
JEM BOO-KOO ey-koo-TAY duh lah mee-ZEEK

I'm a big fan of pizza.
Je suis un grand fan de pizza.
JUH swee uhn grohn fahn duh PEE-tsa

I'm crazy about watching movies.
Je suis fou de regarder des films.
JUH swee foo duh ruh-gar-DAY day feelm

I adore spending time with my friends.
J'adore passer du temps avec mes amis.
ZHAD-OR pah-SAY duh TAHN av-ek may zah-MEE

I'm passionate about cooking.
Je suis passionné de cuisine.
JUH swee pah-see-oh-NAY duh kwee-ZEEN

I'm fond of traveling to new places.
J'aime voyager dans de nouveaux endroits.
JEM vwah-yah-JAY dahn duh noo-voh ZAN-dwah

I really like playing video games.
J'aime beaucoup jouer aux jeux vidéo.
JEM BOO-KOO zhoo-ay oh zhay vee-day-oh

I enjoy going for a walk in nature.
J'aime me promener dans la nature.
JEM pruh-muh-NAY dahn lah nah-TYUR

I'm into reading books.
Je suis passionné de lecture.
JUH swee pah-see-oh-NAY duh luhk-TYUR

I hate getting up early in the morning.
Je déteste me lever tôt le matin.
JUH day-TEST muh luh-VAY troh luh ma-TAN

I can't stand spicy food.
Je ne supporte pas la nourriture épicée.
JUH nuh soor-PORT pah lah noo-ree-TOOR ay-pee-SAY

I'm not a fan of horror movies.
Je ne suis pas fan de films d'horreur.
JUH nuh swee pah fahn duh feelm doh-RUHR

I really dislike being stuck in traffic.
Je déteste être coincé dans le trafic.
JUH day-TEST ay-truh kwan-SAY dahn luh tra-FEEK

I'm not fond of cleaning the house.
Je ne suis pas fan de nettoyer la maison.
JUH nuh swee pah fahn duh nuh-twah-YAY lah may-ZON

I hate doing the dishes.
Je déteste faire la vaisselle.
JUH day-TEST fayr lah vay-ZELL

I'm not into sports.
Je ne suis pas intéressé par les sports.
JUH nuh swee pah an-tay-ray-SAY pahr lay spor

I'm not a fan of crowded places.
Je ne suis pas fan des endroits bondés.
JUH nuh swee pah fahn dayz ahn-dwah bawn-DAY

I don't like taking risks.
Je n'aime pas prendre de risques.
JUH nehm pah pruhn-druh deh reesk

I'm not keen on public speaking.
Je ne suis pas fan de parler en public.
JUH nuh swee pah fahn duh pah-LAY ahn pu-bleek

I enjoy spending time outdoors.
J'aime passer du temps en plein air.
JEM pah-SAYR dew tahN ahn plehn air.

I love playing with my pets.
J'adore jouer avec mes animaux de compagnie.
JAH-dor zhweh ah-vek mayz ah-nee-MOH duh kawn-pahn-YEH.

I'm a fan of classical music.
Je suis une fan de musique classique.
Juh swee zuhn fahn duh moo-ZEEK klah-SEEK.

I'm passionate about dancing.
Je suis passionnée de danse.
Juh swee pah-see-oh-NAY duh dahnss.

I really like watching sunsets.
J'aime beaucoup regarder les couchers de soleil.
JEM boh-koo rahr-duh-zhay lay koo-shay duh soh-lay.

I enjoy painting and drawing.
J'aime peindre et dessiner.
JEM pan-druh ay dess-ee-nay.

I'm into trying new foods.
J'aime essayer de nouveaux plats.
JEM es-say-yay duh noo-vo plah.

I'm a big fan of coffee.
Je suis une grande amateurtrice de café.
Juh swee zuhn grahn dah-ma-turetrice duh kah-FAY.

I love going to the beach.
J'adore aller à la plage.
JAH-dor ah-layr ah lah plahzh.

153

I'm crazy about shopping.
Je suis fou/folle de shopping.
Juh swee foo/fahl duh shopping.

I can't stand being in a noisy environment.
Je ne supporte pas être dans un environnement bruyant.
Juh nuh soh-por-tuh pahz etruh dahN uhN ahN-vee-rohn-mahn brrr-wah-yahN.

I really dislike cleaning up after a party.
Je déteste vraiment ranger après une soirée.
Juh day-tes-tuh vray-mahn rahn-jay ah-preh ewn swah-ray.

I'm not a fan of horror stories.
Je ne suis pas fan des histoires d'horreur.
Juh nuh swee pah fahn dayz ee-stwahr duh-rur.

I hate when my plans get cancelled.
Je déteste quand mes plans sont annulés.
Juh day-tes-tuh kahN may plahN sohN ah-nuh-lay.

I'm not fond of spicy food.
Je ne suis pas fan de la nourriture épicée.
Juh nuh swee pah fahn duh noo-ree-TOO-r ay-pee-SAY.

I don't like being stuck indoors for too long.
Je n'aime pas rester enfermée à l'intérieur trop longtemps.
Juh nem pah res-tayr ah-fair-maye ah laN-teh-ree-uh troh lohN-tahN.

I'm not into watching sports on TV.
Je ne suis pas intéressée par regarder les sports à la télévision.
Juh nuh swee pah ahN-teh-reh-saye pahr rahr-duh lay spohr ah lah teh-lay-vee-zee-yohn.

I'm not keen on horror movies.
Je ne suis pas passionnée par les films d'horreur.
Juh nuh swee pah pah-see-oh-naye pahr lay feelm dor-rur.

I'm not fond of cold weather.
Je n'aime pas le temps froid.
Juh nem pah luh tahN fwa.

I really dislike waiting in long lines.
Je déteste vraiment attendre dans de longues files d'attente.
Juh day-tes-tuh vray-mahn ah-tahnd-ruh dahN duh lohng feel dah-tahnt.

EXPRESSING AGREEMENT AND DISAGREEMENT

I completely agree with you.
Je suis tout à fait d'accord avec vous.
zhuh swee too tah fay dah-KOR ah-vek voo

That's exactly what I was thinking.
C'est exactement ce que je pensais.
seh TEK-seuh-men suh kuh zhuh pahn-SAY

You make a good point.
Vous avez raison.
Voo za-VAY ray-ZON

I couldn't agree more.
Vous avez bien raison.
Voo za-VAY byan ray-ZON

Absolutely!
Absolument!
Ab-so-loo-mahn

That's just what I was about to say.
C'est exactement ce que j'allais dire.
Seh TEK-seuh-men suh zhuh-LAY deer

I'm with you on this.
Je suis d'accord avec vous sur ce point.
Zhuh swee dah-KOR ah-vek voo sur suh pwahn

I'm on the same page.
Nous sommes sur la même longueur d'onde.
Noo sohm sur lah mehm lon-GUHR dohnd

I'm in complete accord.
Je suis en accord complet.
Zhuh swee ahn ah-KOR kohm-PLAY

That makes perfect sense.
Ça a tout son sens.
Sah ah too sohn sahns

You've convinced me.
Vous m'avez convaincu.
Voo mah-VAY kohn-VEHN-koo

You're absolutely right.
Vous avez tout à fait raison.
Voo za-VAY too tah fay ray-ZON

I fully support your position.
Je soutiens pleinement votre position.
Zhuh soo-TEEN ply-nuh-mahn voh-truh po-zee-syon

You have my full agreement.
Vous avez mon entière approbation.
Voo za-VAY mohn ahn-tee-yehr a-proo-ba-syon

I couldn't have said it better myself.
Je n'aurais pas pu mieux le dire moi-même.
Zhuh noh-reh pah puh myuh luh deer mwa-mehm

I'm in complete alignment with your thinking.
Je suis en parfait accord avec votre façon de penser.
Zhuh swee ahn pahr-fay ah-KOR ah-vek vo-truh fah-sawn duh pahn-SAY

That's exactly my thinking too.
C'est exactement ce que je pense aussi.
Seh TEK-seuh-men suh kuh pahn-SAY oh-see

You've articulated my thoughts perfectly.
Vous avez parfaitement exprimé mes pensées.
Voo za-VAY pahr-fay-tuh-mahn ehk-speh-ree-meh meh pahn-SAY

I agree with you one hundred percent.
Je suis d'accord avec vous à cent pour cent.
Zhuh swee dah-KOR ah-vek voo ah sahn poor sahn

You have my vote.
Vous avez mon vote.
Voo za-VAY mohn voht

I'm afraid I have to disagree.
Je crains de devoir être en désaccord.
Zhuh KRAN duh duh-VWAR et-truh an day-za-KOR

I see things differently.
Je vois les choses différemment.
Zhuh vwar lay SHOZ deh-fay-ray-MON

I'm not so sure about that.
Je ne suis pas si sûr de cela.
Zhuh nuh SWEE pah see sur duh suh-LA

I don't think that's right.
Je ne pense pas que ce soit correct.
Zhuh nuh PONSS pah kuh suh SWAH kor-REKT

That's not how I see it.
Ce n'est pas ainsi que je le vois.
Suh NAY pah zan-SEE kuh zhuh luh VWAH

I'm sorry, but I don't agree.
Je suis désolée, mais je ne suis pas d'accord.
Zhuh swee day-zoh-LAY, may zhuh nuh swee pah da-KOR

I respectfully disagree.
Je suis en désaccord avec respect.
Zhuh swee en day-za-KOR a-vek ruh-SPEH

I beg to differ.
Je me permets de différer.
Zhuh muh PEHR-may duh dif-fay-RAY

I'm not convinced.
Je ne suis pas convaincue.
Zhuh nuh swee pah kon-VEN-kuh

That's not my understanding.
Ce n'est pas ce que je comprends.
Suh NAY pah suh kuh zhuh kohn-prawn

I don't think that's accurate.
Je ne pense pas que cela soit précis.
Zhuh nuh PONSS pah kuh suh-LA swah pray-SEES

I don't think that's the case.
Je ne pense pas que cela soit le cas.
Zhuh nuh PONSS pah kuh suh-LA swah luh KAH

I have a different perspective.
J'ai une perspective différente.
Zhay ewn PERS-pehk-TEEV dee-fay-raynt

I don't share your view.
Je ne partage pas votre point de vue.
Zhuh nuh par-TAHZH pah vo-tre pwahn duh VU

That's not what I believe.
Ce n'est pas ce que je crois.
Suh NAY pah suh kuh zhuh KRWAH

I don't think we're on the same page.
Je ne pense pas que nous soyons sur la même longueur d'onde.
Zhuh nuh PONSS pah kuh noo swah-yohn sur luh mem lon-GUHR dond

I'm not comfortable with that idea.
Je ne suis pas à l'aise avec cette idée.
Zhuh nuh swee pah ah LAYZ a-vek set-TEH ee-DAY

That's not my experience.
Ce n'est pas mon expérience.
Zuh NAY pah mohn ayk-SPAY-ree-ahns

I think we need to consider other options.
Je pense que nous devons considérer d'autres options.
Zhuh PONSS kuh noo duh-VOHN kohn-si-day-RAY do-truhz op-SEE-yohn

I have to disagree with you there.
Je dois être en désaccord avec vous à ce sujet.
Zhuh dwahz e-truh an day-za-KOR a-vek voo ah suh sjuh

I can't say I agree.
Je ne peux pas dire que je suis d'accord.
Zhuh nuh puh pah deer kuh zhuh swee dah-KOR

I'm not sure that's the best approach.
Je ne suis pas sûr que ce soit la meilleure approche.
Zhuh nuh swee pah sur kuh suh SWAH lah meh-yor a-prosh

I don't think that's feasible.
Je ne pense pas que cela soit réalisable.
Zuh nuh PONSS pah kuh suh-LA swah reh-al-ee-ZABL

I'm not convinced that's the right solution.
Je ne suis pas convaincu que c'est la bonne solution.
Zhuh nuh swee pah kon-van-KU kuh say lah bawn so-loo-see-yohn

I don't think we should move forward with that.
Je ne pense pas que nous devrions aller de l'avant avec cela.
Zhuh nuh PONSS pah kuh noo duh-vwahr-YOHN al-lay duh sah-lah

I'm not completely sold on that idea.
Je ne suis pas complètement convaincu de cette idée.
Zhuh nuh swee pah kohn-pleh-MAHN kon-van-KU duh set-TEH ee-DAY

I'm hesitant to agree.
Je suis hésitante à être d'accord.
Zhuh swee-EEZ ay-treh day-za-KOR

I'm not sure that's the right course of action.
Je ne suis pas sûr que ce soit le bon choix d'action.
Zhuh nuh swee pah sur kuh suh-LA luh bohn shwah dahk-SEE-yohn

I'm skeptical about that.
Je suis sceptique à ce sujet.
Zhuh swee sep-TEEK a suh sjuh

I think we need to explore other possibilities.
Je pense que nous devons explorer d'autres possibilités.
Zhuh PONSS kuh noo duh-VOHN eks-ploh-RAY do-truhz
pos-see-bee-lee-TAY

MAKING EXCUSES

I'm sorry, but I can't make it today.
Je suis désolée, mais je ne peux pas venir aujourd'hui.
Zhuh swee day-ZOH-lay, may zhuh nuh puh vuh-NEER oh-zhoor-DWEE

I can't come to the party because I have to work late.
Je ne peux pas venir à la fête parce que je dois travailler tard.
Zhuh nuh puh vuh-NEER ah la FET pahrskuh zhuh dwah trah-vah-YAY tar

I can't meet you because I have a prior engagement.
Je ne peux pas te rencontrer parce que j'ai un engagement préalable.
Zhuh nuh puh tuh rawn-kawn-TRAY pahrskuh zhay uhN ahn-gaj-MOHN pray-ah-LAHBL

I'm sorry, but I'm feeling under the weather.
Je suis désolée, mais je ne me sens pas bien.
Zhuh swee day-ZOH-lay, may zhuh nuh muh sahN pah bee-EN

I can't go out tonight because I'm really tired.
Je ne peux pas sortir ce soir parce que je suis très fatiguée.
Zhuh nuh puh sohr-TEER suh SWAHR pahrskuh zhuh swee TRAY fah-tee-GAY

I can't make it to the meeting because of a family emergency.
Je ne peux pas assister à la réunion à cause d'une urgence familiale.
Zhuh nuh puh ah-SEE-stay ah lah ray-YOHN ah kohz DUHN oor-jahNS fah-mee-LYAL

I can't attend the conference because of a scheduling conflict.
Je ne peux pas assister à la conférence à cause d'un conflit d'emploi du temps.
Zhuh nuh puh ah-SEE-stay ah lah kohn-FAY-rohNS ah kohz DUHn kohn-FLEE dahn-plwah duh tahn

I can't go to the gym today because I have a headache.
Je ne peux pas aller au gym aujourd'hui parce que j'ai mal à la tête.
Zhuh nuh puh ah-LAY oh zheem oh-zhoor-DWEE pahrskuh zhay mah-lah-TET

I can't help you move because I have a doctor's appointment.
Je ne peux pas t'aider à déménager parce que j'ai un rendez-vous chez le médecin.
Zhuh nuh puh teh-DAY ah DAY-muh-NAH-jay pahrskuh zhay uh rawn-day-voo shay luh may-duh-SAN

I can't go out for drinks tonight because I have to study.
Je ne peux pas sortir prendre un verre ce soir parce que je dois étudier.
Zhuh nuh puh sohr-TEER prahn-dr uh vehr suh SWAHR pahrskuh zhuh dwah ay-tew-DY-ay

I can't come to the dinner party because I'm going out of town.
Je ne peux pas venir à la soirée dînatoire car je pars en voyage.
Zhuh nuh puh vuh-NEER ah lah swa-ray DEE-na-twahr kar zhuh par awn voy-AJ

I'm sorry, but I can't go to the game because I have other plans.
Je suis désolée, mais je ne peux pas aller au match car j'ai d'autres projets.
Zhuh swee day-ZOH-lay, may zhuh nuh puh ah-LAY oh mahsh kar zhay doh-tr proh-JAY

I can't attend the event because I have a prior commitment.
Je ne peux pas assister à l'événement car j'ai un engagement préalable.
Zhuh nuh puh ah-SEE-stay ah lay-VAY-nuh-mawn kar zhay uhN ahn-gaj-MOHN pray-ah-LAHBL

I can't go to the concert because I can't afford the ticket.
Je ne peux pas aller au concert car je ne peux pas me permettre le billet.
Zhuh nuh puh ah-LAY oh kohn-SAIR kar zhuh nuh puh muh pahr-MEHT-truh luh bee-YAY

I can't attend the wedding because I have to work that day.
Je ne peux pas assister au mariage car je dois travailler ce jour-là.
Zhuh nuh puh ah-SEE-stay oh ma-ree-AJ kar zhuh dwah trah-vah-YAY suh jooR-lah

I can't make it to the appointment because of a personal emergency.
Je ne peux pas être présente à mon rendez-vous à cause d'une urgence personnelle.
Zhuh nuh puh ET-truh pray-ZAWNT ah mawn rawN-day-voo ah kohz DUHN oor-jahNS per-soh-NELL

I can't join you for lunch because I already have plans.
Je ne peux pas déjeuner avec toi car j'ai déjà des projets.
Zhuh nuh puh day-zhuh-NAY ah-vehk twa kar zhay day-ZHAH day proh-JAY

I'm sorry, but I can't participate in the project because of a conflict of interest.
Je suis désolée, mais je ne peux pas participer au projet en raison d'un conflit d'intérêts.
Zhuh swee day-ZOH-lay, may zhuh nuh puh par-tis-ee-pay oh pro-jay ahn ray-ZON duhn kohn-FLEE dahN-teh-RAY

I can't go to the movies because I have a deadline to meet.
Je ne peux pas aller au cinéma car j'ai une échéance à respecter.
Zhuh nuh puh ah-LAY oh see-NAY-mah kar zhay yewN ay-SHAY-ahNs ah res-peh-TEH

I can't go out for dinner because I have to finish some work.
Je ne peux pas sortir dîner car je dois finir du travail.
Zhuh nuh puh sohr-TEER DEE-nay kar zhuh dwah fin-NEER dew trah-vah-YAY

I can't come to the party because I have a family gathering.
Je ne peux pas venir à la fête parce que j'ai une réunion de famille.
ZHUH nuh puh pah ven-EER ah lah fett pahrskuh zhay ewn ruh-yun-yon duh fam-yuh

I can't attend the meeting because of a scheduling conflict.
Je ne peux pas assister à la réunion en raison d'un conflit d'emploi du temps.
ZHUH nuh puh ah-see-TEH ah lah ray-yoon-yon ahn ray-zon dun kon-flee duh ahm-pwah

I can't make it to the interview because of transportation issues.
Je ne peux pas me rendre à l'entretien à cause de problèmes de transport.
ZHUH nuh puh muh rahn-druh ah lah on-treh-tee-EN ah kohz duh praw-blem duh trahn-spor

I can't go on the trip because of a financial constraint.
Je ne peux pas partir en voyage à cause d'une contrainte financière.
ZHUH nuh puh pahr-TEER ahn voy-ahzh ah kohz duhn kon-trant fan-see-air

I can't go to the gym because I'm not feeling well.
Je ne peux pas aller à la salle de gym car je ne me sens pas bien.
ZHUH nuh puh ah-lay ah lah sal duh zheem kahr zhuh nuh muh sahn pah byan

I can't help you move because I have a previous engagement.
Je ne peux pas vous aider à déménager car j'ai un engagement antérieur.
ZHUH nuh puh voo zay-day ah day-meh-nah-zhay kahr zhay ewn ahn-gaj-mahn an-tye-ryeure

I can't attend the concert because I have another commitment.
Je ne peux pas assister au concert car j'ai un autre engagement.
ZHUH nuh puh ah-see-TEH o kon-sair kahr zhay ewn oh-truh an-gaj-mahn

I can't participate in the project because of a lack of expertise.
Je ne peux pas participer au projet à cause d'un manque d'expertise.
ZHUH nuh puh pahr-tee-see-pay oh pro-jay ah kohz dun mahnk deks-peer-tees

I can't come to the party because I have to study for an exam.
Je ne peux pas venir à la fête car je dois étudier pour un examen.
ZHUH nuh puh ven-EER ah lah fett kahr zhuh dwah zeh-tyuh-dee-yay poor un eg-zah-mahn

I can't make it to the conference because of a health issue.
Je ne peux pas assister à la conférence à cause d'un problème de santé.
ZHUH nuh puh ah-see-TEH ah lah kohn-fay-ronce ah kohz dun praw-blem duh sahntay

ASKING AND GIVING PERMISSION

Can I borrow your pen, please?
Puis-je emprunter votre stylo, s'il vous plaît ?
PUIS-JUH ahm-PRAWN-TER VOTR stee-LOH, SEEL VOUS PLAIT?

May I use your phone for a minute?
Puis-je utiliser votre téléphone pour une minute, s'il vous plaît ?
PUIS-JUH oo-TEE-LEE-ZEH VOTR tay-lay-FOHN poor oon meen-UTE, SEEL VOUS PLAIT?

Would it be okay if I left early today?
Serait-ce possible que je parte plus tôt aujourd'hui, s'il vous plaît ?
SE-REH suh POSS-EE-BL ker juh PART plu toh OH-jur-DWEE, SEEL VOUS PLAIT?

Is it alright if I take a break now?
Est-ce que cela vous dérange si je prends une pause maintenant, s'il vous plaît ?
ESK suh suh-LAH voo DE-RAHNJ see juh PRAWN oon pohz main-NUHNT, SEEL VOUS PLAIT?

Can I ask you a personal question?
Puis-je vous poser une question personnelle, s'il vous plaît ?
PUIS-JUH voo po-ZEHR oon kess-TYOHN per-soh-NEHL, SEEL VOUS PLAIT?

May I open the window, please?
Puis-je ouvrir la fenêtre, s'il vous plaît ?
PUIS-JUH ooh-VREER lah fuh-NETR, SEEL VOUS PLAIT?

Do you mind if I turn on the music?
Est-ce que cela vous dérange si j'allume la musique, s'il vous plaît ?
ESK suh suh-LAH voo DE-RAHNJ see zhah-LUHM lah moo-ZEEK, SEEL VOUS PLAIT?

Would it be okay if I brought a friend along?
Serait-il possible d'amener un ami avec moi, s'il vous plaît ?
SE-REH-TEEL POSS-EE-BL DAM-NAY oon ah-MEE ah-VEK MWAA, SEEL VOUS PLAIT?

Could I take a day off next week?
Serait-il possible que je prenne un jour de congé la semaine prochaine, s'il vous plaît ?
SE-REH-TEEL POSS-EE-BL ker juh PREHN uhn zhoor duh kon-ZHAY lah sem-ANE pro-SHEN, SEEL VOUS PLAIT?

Can I leave my bag here for a moment?
Puis-je laisser mon sac ici pour un moment, s'il vous plaît ?
PUIS-JUH LEH-sehr mohN sak ee-SEE poor un mo-MAHN, SEEL VOUS PLAIT?

May I take a picture of this artwork?
Puis-je prendre une photo de cette œuvre d'art, s'il vous plaît ?
PUIS-JUH PRAHND-ruhn PHO-toh duh SET oovr-dar, SEEL VOUS PLAIT?

Would it be okay if I changed the channel?
Est-ce que cela vous dérange si je change de chaîne, s'il vous plaît ?
ESK suh suh-LAH voo DE-RAHNJ see zhuh shanzh duh SHAIN, SEEL VOUS PLAIT?

Is it alright if I smoke here?
Est-ce que cela vous dérange si je fume ici, s'il vous plaît ?
ESK suh suh-LAH voo DE-RAHNJ see zhuh fyoom ee-SEE, SEEL VOUS PLAIT?

Do you mind if I close the door?
Est-ce que cela vous dérange si je ferme la porte, s'il vous plaît ?
ESK suh suh-LAH voo DE-RAHNJ see zhuh FER-muh la PORTE, SEEL VOUS PLAIT?

Sure, go ahead and borrow my pen.
Bien sûr, empruntez mon stylo.
BYAN-SUR, ahm-PRAWN-TEH MON stee-LOH.

Yes, you may use my phone for a minute.
Oui, vous pouvez utiliser mon téléphone pour une minute.
WEE, voo POO-VAY ootee-lee-ZEH MON tay-lay-FOHN poor oon meen-UTE.

Of course, it's okay if you leave early today.
Bien sûr, vous pouvez partir plus tôt aujourd'hui.
BYAN-SUR, voo POO-VAY PAR-TEER plu toh OH-jur-DWEE.

Yes, you can take a break now.
Oui, vous pouvez prendre une pause maintenant.
WEE, voo POO-VAY PRAWN-druhn oon POHZ main-NUHNT.

Yes, go ahead and ask me a personal question.
Oui, allez-y et posez-moi une question personnelle.
WEE, ah-LAY-ZEE eh po-ZEH-MWAH oon kess-TYOHN per-soh-NEHL.

Certainly, you may open the window.
Bien sûr, vous pouvez ouvrir la fenêtre.
BYAN-SUR, voo POO-VAY oo-vreeR la fuh-NEHT-ruh.

Sure, you can turn on the music.
Bien sûr, vous pouvez allumer la musique.
BYAN-SUR, voo POO-VAY ah-LOO-may la mew-ZEEK.

Yes, it's okay if you bring a friend along.
Oui, vous pouvez amener un ami avec vous.
WEE, voo POO-VAY AH-muh-nay uh-NA-mee ah-VEK voo.

Of course, you can take a day off next week.
Bien sûr, vous pouvez prendre un jour de congé la semaine prochaine.
BYAN-SUR, voo POO-VAY PRAWN-druhn zhoor duh kon-ZHAY la seman pro-SHEN.

Yes, you may leave your bag here for a moment.
Oui, vous pouvez laisser votre sac ici pour un moment.
WEE, voo POO-VAY LEH-sehr vo-tre sahk ee-SEE poor un mo-MAHN.

Yes, you may take a picture of this artwork.
Oui, vous pouvez prendre une photo de cette œuvre d'art.
WEE, voo POO-VAY PRAWN-druhn oon PHO-toh duh SET oovr-dar.

Sure, go ahead and change the channel.
Bien sûr, allez-y et changez de chaîne.
BYAN-SUR, ah-LAY-ZEE eh shanzh duh SHAINJ.

Yes, you may have a sip of my water.
Oui, vous pouvez prendre une gorgée de mon eau.
WEE, voo POO-VAY PRAWN-druhn oon gor-JAY duh moh noh.

Yes, it's alright if you smoke here.
Oui, cela ne me dérange pas si vous fumez ici.
WEE, suh-LAH nuh muh DE-RAHNZH pah see voo fyoo-MEH ee-SEE.

Of course, you can close the door.
Bien sûr, vous pouvez fermer la porte.
BYAN-SUR, voo POO-VAY FEHR-MAY la PORTE.

MAKING COMPARISONS

How does this compare to that?
Comment cela se compare-t-il à cela?
Koh-mahn suh-LAH kuhm-PAH-ruh-teel ah suh-LAH?

Which one do you think is better?
Lequel pensez-vous est meilleur?
Luh-KEHL pahn-SEH-voo eh muh-YEUR?

In what ways are these two things alike or different?
De quelles façons ces deux choses sont-elles similaires ou différentes?
Duh KEHL fah-SOH ceh DEUH shoh-SOH sohn-TEHL sim-eel-YAIR ooh DEE-feh-RENTE?

Which one do you prefer, X or Y?
Lequel préférez-vous, X ou Y?
Luh-KEHL pray-feh-REH-voo, eeks oo eegrek?

What are the advantages and disadvantages of each option?
Quels sont les avantages et les inconvénients de chaque option?
Kell sohn lay-VAHN-tahj lay zahn-kohN-vay-nyahn duh shahk OH-pee-yohn?

What are the pros and cons of each alternative?
Quels sont les avantages et les inconvénients de chaque alternative?
Kell sohn lay-VAHN-tahj lay zahn-kohN-vay-nyahn duh shahk ahl-tair-nah-TEEV?

*Insert X and Y with the applicable person, place or thing you wish to compare.

X is bigger than Y.
X est plus grand que Y.
Eks eh ploo grahN kuh EE-grek.

Y is smaller than X.
Y est plus petit que X.
EE-grek eh ploo puh-TEE kuh EE.

X is heavier than Y.
X est plus lourd que Y.
Eks eh ploo loor kuh EE.

Y is lighter than X.
Y est plus léger que X.
EE eh ploo lay-ZHAY kuh eks.

X is faster than Y.
X est plus rapide que Y.
Eks eh ploo rah-PEED kuh EE.

Y is slower than X.
Y est plus lent que X.
EE eh ploo lahn kuh eks.

X is stronger than Y.
X est plus fort que Y.
Eks eh ploo fohr kuh EE.

Y is weaker than X.
Y est plus faible que X.
EE eh ploo fay-bl kuh eks.

X is better than Y.
X est meilleur que Y.
Eks eh muh-YEUR kuh EE-grek.

Y is worse than X.
Y est pire que X.
EE-grek eh peer kuh eks.

X is more beautiful than Y.
X est plus beau/belle que Y.
Eks eh ploo boh/BEHL kuh EE.

Y is less beautiful than X.
Y est moins beau/belle que X.
EE eh mwahn boh/BEHL kuh eks.

X is taller than Y.
X est plus grand que Y.
Eks eh ploo grahN kuh EE.

Y is shorter than X.
Y est plus petit que X.
EE-grek eh ploo puh-TEE kuh eks.

X is more intelligent than Y.
X est plus intelligent que Y.
Eks eh ploo an-tee-leezh-AHN kuh EE.

X is more talented than Y.
X est plus talentueux/talentueuse que Y.
Eks eh ploo tah-lahn-TEU/TEUZ kuh EE.

Y is less talented than X.
Y est moins talentueux/talentueuse que X.
EE-grek eh mwahn tah-lahn-TEU/TEUZ kuh eks.

X is more interesting than Y.
X est plus intéressant(e) que Y.
Eks eh ploo an-tay-ray-SAHNT kuh EE.

Y is less interesting than X.
Y est moins intéressant(e) que X.
EE-grek eh mwahn an-tay-ray-SAHNT kuh eks.

X is more exciting than Y.
X est plus excitant(e) que Y.
Eks eh ploo eks-see-TAHNT kuh EE.

Y is less exciting than X.
Y est moins excitant(e) que X.
EE-grek eh mwahn eks-see-TAHNT kuh eks.

X is more fun than Y.

X est plus amusant(e) que Y.

Eks eh ploo ah-mew-ZAHNT kuh EE.

Y is less fun than X.

Y est moins amusant(e) que X.

EE-grek eh mwahn ah-mew-ZAHNT kuh eks.

X is more expensive than Y.

X est plus cher que Y.

Eks eh ploo shehr kuh EE.

Y is less expensive than X.

Y est moins cher que X.

EE-grek eh mwahn shehr kuh eks.

X is more affordable than Y.

X est plus abordable que Y.

Eks eh ploo ah-bohr-dahbl kuh EE.

Y is less affordable than X.

Y est moins abordable que X.

EE-grek eh mwahn ah-bohr-dahbl kuh eks.

EXPRESSING GRATITUDE AND APOLOGIES

Thank you so much!
Merci beaucoup !
MEHR-see boh-KOO !

Thanks for being there for me.
Merci d'avoir été là pour moi.
MEHR-see dah-vwahr ay LAH poor mwah.

I can't thank you enough.
Je ne peux pas assez te remercier.
Zhuh nuh puh pah ah-SAY tuh ruh-mehr-see-yay.

Thank you for your kindness.
Merci pour votre gentillesse.
MEHR-see poor vo-truh zhawn-TEE-yes.

Thank you from the bottom of my heart.
Merci du fond de mon cœur.
MEHR-see dew fohn duh mohn ker.

Thanks a million!
Merci mille fois!
MEHR-see meel fwah!

I'm sorry.
Je suis désolé(e).
Zhuh swee day-zoh-LAY.

I apologize.
Je m'excuse.
Zhuh mehk-SKYUZ.

Please forgive me.
S'il vous plaît pardonnez-moi.
Seel voo pleh pahr-doh-nay-MWAH.

I take full responsibility.
Je prends l'entière responsabilité.
Zhuh prahn lon-tee-air ruh-spohn-sah-bee-li-tay.

I regret my actions.
Je regrette mes actions.
Zhuh ruh-gret muh-zack-see-yawn.

I didn't mean to hurt you.
Je ne voulais pas te faire de mal.
Zhuh nuh voo-lay pah tuh fair duh mahl.

I promise to make it up to you.
Je promets de me rattraper.
Zhuh proh-MET duh muh ra-treh-pay.

I understand if you don't forgive me.
Je comprends si vous ne me pardonnez pas.
Zhuh kohn-prahn-DS see voo nuh muh pahr-doh-nay pah.

I really appreciate your help.
Je suis vraiment reconnaissant(e) de votre aide.
Zhuh swee vr-eh-man ruh-koh-nay-SAHNT duh vo-truh ed.

I can't thank you enough for what you've done.
Je ne pourrai jamais assez vous remercier pour ce que vous avez fait.
Zhuh nuh poor-ray zhuh-may ah-SAY voo ruh-mehr-see-yay poor suh kuh voo zah-vay fay.

You have my sincere gratitude.
Vous avez ma sincère gratitude.
VOO zah-veh ma san-SEHR grah-ti-TOOD.

I'm so grateful for your kindness.
Je suis tellement reconnaissant de votre gentillesse.
Zhuh swee TELL-mahn ruh-kuh-NEH-sahn duh VOT-ruh zhan-TEE-YES.

I'm truly thankful for your support.
Je suis vraiment reconnaissant de votre soutien.
Zhuh swee vruh-MAHN ruh-kuh-NEH-sahn duh VOT-ruh soo-TYEH.

I can't express how grateful I am.
Je ne peux pas exprimer à quel point je suis reconnaissant.
Zhuh nuh puh pahk-spree-MAY ah kell PWAHN zhuh swee ruh-kuh-NEH-sahn.

I'm indebted to you for your generosity.
Je vous suis redevable pour votre générosité.
Zhuh VOO swee ruh-duh-VABLUH poor VOT-ruh zhen-ay-roh-zee-TAY.

I'm blessed to have you in my life.
Je suis béni de vous avoir dans ma vie.
Zhuh swee beh-NEE duh VOOZ ah-VWAR dan mah VEE.

Your help has been invaluable to me.
Votre aide a été inestimable pour moi.
VOT-ruh ED ah eh-tay een-es-tee-MAHBL poor mwah.

You're a true lifesaver, thank you.
Vous êtes un véritable sauveur, merci.
VOO ZET uh vey-teh-bluh soh-vuhr, mair-SEE.

I'll never forget your kindness.
Je n'oublierai jamais votre gentillesse.
Zhuh noo-blee-RAY zhuh-MAIR VOT-ruh zhan-TEE-YES.

I'm so fortunate to have you as a friend.
Je suis tellement chanceux de vous avoir comme ami(e).
Zhuh swee TELL-mahn shon-SUH de VOOZ ah-VWAR kohm AH-mee.

Your assistance means the world to me.
Votre assistance signifie le monde pour moi.
VOT-ruh ah-SEE-stahns see-nee-fee leh mohnd poor mwah.

I'm touched by your thoughtfulness.
Je suis touché(e) par votre prévenance.
Zhuh swee too-SHAY par VOT-ruh pray-vnuhns.

I'm grateful for your understanding.
Je suis reconnaissant de votre compréhension.
Zhuh swee ruh-kno-SAN duh vo-treh kom-preh-an-SION

Thank you for your time.
Merci pour votre temps.
Mehr-SEE poor vo-treh TOM

You're a lifesaver!
Vous êtes un sauveur!
Voo zet uh so-vuhr

I'm grateful for your guidance.
Je suis reconnaissant de votre guidage.
Zhuh swee ruh-kno-SAN duh vo-treh gee-DAZH

Thanks for making a difference.
Merci de faire la différence.
Mehr-SEE duh fair lah dee-fay-RAHNS

I can't express my gratitude enough.
Je ne peux pas exprimer suffisamment ma gratitude.
Zhuh nuh puh pahz ex-pree-may soo-fi-za-mohn ma gra-ti-TUDE

You're a wonderful person.
Vous êtes une personne merveilleuse.
Voo zet uhnuh pair-SONN mehr-vay-YEUZ

I'm blessed to know you.
Votre gentillesse ne sera jamais oubliée.
Vo-treh zhon-tee-yes nuh se-ra zhuh-mayz oo-blee-YAY

Your kindness will never be forgotten.
Je suis béni de vous connaître.
Zhuh swee bey-NEE duh voo co-nai-TRE

Thank you for being you.
Merci d'être vous-même.
Mehr-SEE detruh voo-mem

I'm sorry for my mistake.
Je suis désolée pour mon erreur.
ZHUH swee day-SO-lay poor mohN ay-REUR.

Please forgive me.
S'il vous plaît, pardonnez-moi.
SEEL VOUS PLAIT, par-doh-nay MWAH.

I didn't mean to hurt you.
Je n'avais pas l'intention de vous blesser.
ZHUH nah-VAY pah lahn-tee-ON duh voo bleh-SAY.

I'm sorry for causing you trouble.
Je suis désolée de vous avoir causé des ennuis.
ZHUH swee day-SO-lay duh voo zah-VWAHR koh-zay day zahn-NWEE.

I regret what I did.
Je regrette ce que j'ai fait.
ZHUH ruh-GRET suh keh zjeh FAY.

I'm sorry for being late.
Je suis désolée d'être en retard.
ZHUH swee day-SO-lay deht-ray ahN ree-YAHR.

Please accept my apologies.
Veuillez accepter mes excuses.
VUH-yay ak-sep-TAY mayz ehk-SKOOZ.

I messed up and I'm sorry.
J'ai merdé et je suis désolée.
ZHAY mehr-DAY ay ZHUH swee day-SO-lay.

I'm deeply sorry for my actions.
Je suis profondément désolée pour mes actions.
ZHUH swee pro-FOH-duh-mahN day-SO-lay poor mayz ahk-see-YOHN.

I apologize for any inconvenience I caused.
Je m'excuse pour tout inconvénient que j'ai pu causer.
ZHUH mex-KUZ poor tooN ahN-kohn-VAY-nyahN kuh zhay puh koh-ZAY.

GIVING AND RECEIVING COMPLIMENTS

You look great today!
Vous avez l'air superbe aujourd'hui !
VOO-zah-veyz layr soo-PERB oh-zhoor-DWEE!

That outfit suits you perfectly.
Cette tenue vous va parfaitement.
SET-tuh TENUH voo vah pahr-feet-mahn.

Your hair looks amazing!
Vos cheveux ont l'air incroyable !
VOHSH shuh-VUH ohnt layr an-kwah-yuhbl!

You have a wonderful smile.
Vous avez un sourire merveilleux.
VOO-zah-veyz un soo-REER muhr-vay-YUH!

You have a great sense of style.
Vous avez un excellent sens du style.
VOO-zah-veyz un ehks-SELL-uhnt sahns doo steehl.

You're so talented at [insert skill].
Vous êtes tellement douée pour [insérer la compétence].
VOOZ-ett TEL-mahn doo-AY poor [in-seh-RAY la KOM-puh-TAHNS].

You did a fantastic job on [insert task/project].
Vous avez fait un travail fantastique sur [insérer la tâche/projet].
VOO-zah-vey fay un trah-VAY fan-tah-STEEK sur [in-seh-RAY la tash/proh-JAY].

You have a beautiful voice.
Vous avez une voix magnifique.
VOO-zah-veyz oon VWAH mag-nee-FEAK.

Your cooking is delicious.
Votre cuisine est délicieuse.
VOH-truh kwee-ZEEN ay day-lee-see-UHZ.

Your presentation was very engaging.
Votre présentation était très captivante.
VOH-truh pray-zan-ta-SYON eh-TAY tray cap-TEE-vahnt.

Your work is always outstanding.
Votre travail est toujours exceptionnel.
VOH-truh trah-VAY ay too-zhoor ehks-sep-syon-ELL.

You have a great sense of humor.
Vous avez un grand sens de l'humour.
VOO-zah-veyz un grahnd sahns duh oo-MOOR.

You're an excellent listener.
Vous êtes une excellente auditeur/trice.
VOOZ-ett uhn ehks-SELL-uhnt oh-dit-TEUR/TREESS.

You have a wonderful personality.
Vous avez une personnalité formidable.
VOO-zah-veyz oon pehr-soh-na-lee-tay fohr-mee-DAHB.

You inspire me.
Vous m'inspirez.
VOO mahn-spee-RAY.

Thank you, that's very kind of you to say.
Merci, c'est très gentil de votre part de dire ça.
MEHR-see, say tray zhan-TEE duh voh-truh pahr duh deer sah.

I really appreciate your compliment.
Je suis vraiment reconnaissante de votre compliment.
Zhuh swee vrE-man ruh-ko-NEH-sahnd duh voh-truh kohm-plee-MAHN.

That means a lot to me, thank you.
Cela signifie beaucoup pour moi, merci.
Suh-LA se-nee-fee BEA-koo poor mwah, MEHR-see.

I'm glad you like it.
Je suis heureux/heureuse que cela vous plaise.
Zhuh swee uh-ruh/uh-ruhz kuh suh-LA voo pleh-ZE.

181

Thank you, you made my day!
Merci, vous avez illuminé ma journée !
MEHR-see, voo-zah-veyz ee-loo-mee-NAY ma zhur-NAY.

I'm flattered, thank you.
Je suis flattée, merci.
Zhuh swee flah-tehM/F, MEHR-see.

You're so sweet, thank you for saying that.
Tu es tellement gentille, merci de dire ça.
Too eh tehl-mahn zhan-teeY/L, MEHR-see duh deer sah.

That's very thoughtful of you to say.
C'est très réfléchi de votre part de dire ça.
Seh tray ray-fleh-SHEE duh voh-truh pahr duh deer sah.

Thank you, I worked hard on it.
Merci, j'ai travaillé dur pour ça.
MEHR-see, zhay trah-vah-LAY dur poor sah.

I'm glad you noticed.
Je suis contente que vous ayez remarqué.
Zhuh swee kohn-tahnM/F kuh voo zeh reh-mahr-KAY.

Thank you, I feel encouraged.
Merci, je me sens encouragée.
MEHR-see, zhuh muh sahns ahn-kou-rah-ZHAY.

You have made me feel proud.
Vous m'avez fait sentir fier/fière.
Voo mah-vey fay san-TEER F/YEHR.

That's so nice of you, thank you.
C'est très gentil de votre part, merci.
Seh tray zhan-TEE duh voh-truh pahr, MEHR-see.

Thank you, you have made me feel appreciated.
Merci, vous m'avez fait sentir appréciée.
MEHR-see, voo mah-vey fay san-TEER ah-pray-syay-AY.

Your words mean a lot to me, thank you.
Vos paroles signifient beaucoup pour moi, merci.
Voh pah-ROLL se-nee-fee BEA-koo poor mwah, MEHR-see.

MAKING PHONE CALLS

Hello, this is [name].
Bonjour, c'est [nom].
BOHN-JOOR, say [nom].

Can I speak to [name], please?
Puis-je parler à [nom], s'il vous plaît ?
PWEEZH PAHR-LEH ah [nom], SEEL VOUS PLAIT?

May I know who's calling?
Puis-je savoir qui appelle ?
PWEEZH SAV-WAHR kee ah-PELL?

Sorry, wrong number.
Désolé, mauvais numéro.
DAY-ZOH-LEH, moh-VAY noo-MEH-ROH.

I'll call you back in a few minutes.
Je vous rappelle dans quelques minutes.
ZHUH VOH rah-PEL dahng kehlk mee-NOOT.

Can you hear me okay?
M'entendez-vous bien ?
MONT-ON-DEH VOO bee-EN?

I have a bad connection, can I call you back?
J'ai une mauvaise connexion, puis-je vous rappeler ?
ZHAY OON moh-VEZ koh-NEK-SEE-ON, PWEEZH VOO rah-PEL-AY?

Thank you for calling.
Merci d'avoir appelé.
MEHR-SEE dav-WAH ah-peh-LAY.

Sorry, I missed your call.
Désolé, j'ai manqué votre appel.
DAY-ZOH-LEH, zhay mahn-KAY voh-truh ah-PEHL.

What's up?
Quoi de neuf ?
KWUH duh NUHF?

How can I help you?
Comment puis-je vous aider ?
KOH-MOHN PWEEZH VOO ZEH-DEH?

I'm returning your call.
Je vous rappelle.
ZHUH VOH rah-PEL.

I'm sorry, I didn't catch that.
Je suis désolé, je n'ai pas compris.
ZHUH SWEE day-ZOH-LEH, zhuh NAY pah kohm-PREE.

Could you repeat that, please?
Pouvez-vous répéter, s'il vous plaît ?
POO-VAY VOO ray-PAY-TAY, SEEL VOUS PLAIT?

Let me check and get back to you.
Laissez-moi vérifier et je vous rappelle.
LAY-SAY MWAH vay-REE-fee-KAY ay zhuh VOO rah-PEL.

Can you hold on for a moment?
Pouvez-vous patienter un instant ?
POO-VAY VOO pah-TEE-AHN-TAY uhng ahn-STAHN?

I need to put you on hold.
Je dois vous mettre en attente.
ZHUH DWAH VOO met-truh ahn ah-TAHNT.

I'll transfer you to the right department.
Je vais vous transférer au bon service.
ZHUH VAY VOO trahnz-FEH-RAY oh bohn sair-VEES.

I'll leave a message for them to call you back.
Je vais laisser un message pour qu'ils vous rappellent.
ZHUH VAY leh-SAY uhn meh-SAJ poor keel voo rah-pell.

185

Sorry, they're not available right now.
Désolé, ils ne sont pas disponibles pour le moment.
DAY-ZOH-LEH, eel nuh sohn pah dee-poh-NEE-bluh poor luh moh-MAHNG.

Can you call me back later?
Pouvez-vous me rappeler plus tard ?
POO-VAY VOO muh rah-PEL-AY ploo tar?

Can I leave a message?
Puis-je laisser un message ?
PWEEZH leh-SAY uhn meh-SAJ?

Thank you for leaving a message.
Merci d'avoir laissé un message.
MEHR-SEE dav-WAH leh-SAY uhn meh-SAJ.

I'll call you back as soon as possible.
Je vous rappellerai dès que possible.
ZHUH VOO rah-pell-er-AY day keuh poh-SEE-bluh.

It was nice talking to you.
C'était agréable de parler avec vous.
SEH-TAY ah-gruh-AB-luh duh pahr-LEH ah-VEK VOO.

Take care, bye.
Prenez soin de vous, au revoir.
PRUH-NAY SWAHN duh VOO, oh ruh-VWAHR.

Goodbye for now.
Au revoir pour le moment.
Oh ruh-VWAHR poor luh moh-MAHNG.

Speak to you soon.
À bientôt.
AH bee-AN-toh.

Have a good day.
Bonne journée.
BON zhur-nay.

Thanks for calling.
Merci de votre appel.
MEHR-SEE duh vo-tre ah-pehl.

DESCRIBING FEELINGS AND EMOTIONS

I am happy.
Je suis heureux/heureuse.
JUH SWEEZ uhr-UH/uhr-UHZ.

I feel joyful.
Je ressens de la joie.
JUH reh-SEHN duh zhwa.

I am excited.
Je suis excité/excitée.
JUH SWEEZ ehk-SEE-teh/ehk-SEE-teh.

I am elated.
Je suis exalté/exaltée.
JUH SWEEZ ehk-SAL-teh/ehk-SAL-teh.

I am content.
Je suis content/contente.
JUH SWEEZ kohn-TAHN/kohn-TAHNT.

I feel at peace.
Je me sens en paix.
JUH muh sahns ahn peh.

I am calm.
Je suis calme.
JUH SWEEZ kahlm.

I feel relaxed.
Je me sens détendu/détendue.
JUH muh sahns deh-tahn-doo/deh-tahn-doo.

I am satisfied.
Je suis satisfait/satisfaite.
JUH SWEEZ sah-tee-FEH/sah-tee-FEET.

I feel fulfilled.
Je me sens accompli/accomplie.
JUH muh sahns ahk-ohm-PLEE/ahk-ohm-PLEE.

I am proud.
Je suis fier/fière.
JUH SWEEZ fyehr/fyehr.

I feel accomplished.
Je me sens accompli/accomplie.
JUH muh sahns ahk-ohm-PLEE/ahk-ohm-PLEE.

I am confident.
Je suis confiant/confiante.
JUH SWEEZ kohn-fee-AHN/kohn-fee-AHNT.

I feel powerful.
Je me sens puissant/puissante.
JUH muh sahns pwih-SAHN/pwih-SAHNT.

I am motivated.
Je suis motivé/motivée.
JUH SWEEZ moh-tee-VAY/moh-tee-VAY.

I feel inspired.
Je suis inspiré/inspirée.
JUH SWEEZ ahn-spee-RAY/ahn-spee-RAY.

I am curious.
Je suis curieux/curieuse.
JUH SWEEZ koo-ryuh/koo-ryuhz.

I feel interested.
Je suis intéressé/intéressée.
JUH SWEEZ ahn-teh-reh-SEH/ahn-teh-reh-SEET.

I am focused.
Je suis concentré/concentrée.
JUH SWEEZ kohn-sahn-TRAY/kohn-sahn-TREE.

I feel determined.
Je suis déterminé/déterminée.
JUH SWEEZ day-tehr-mee-NAY/day-tehr-mee-NEE.

I am hopeful.
Je suis plein d'espoir.
JUH SWEEZ plahn deh-SPWAHR.

I feel optimistic.
Je suis optimiste.
JUH SWEEZ ohp-teh-MIST.

I am grateful.
Je suis reconnaissant/reconnaissante.
JUH SWEEZ ruh-koh-nay-SAHN/ruh-koh-nay-SAHT.

I feel thankful.
Je suis reconnaissant/reconnaissante.
JUH SWEEZ ruh-koh-nay-SAHN/ruh-koh-nay-SAHT.

I am touched.
Je suis ému/émue.
JUH SWEEZ ay-moo/ay-mew.

I feel moved.
Je suis ému/émue.
JUH SWEEZ ay-moo/ay-mew.

I am empathetic.
Je suis empathique.
JUH SWEEZ ahm-pah-TEEK.

I feel compassionate.
Je suis compatissant/compatissante.
JUH SWEEZ kohm-pah-tee-SAHN/kohm-pah-tee-SAHT.

I am understanding.
Je suis compréhensif/compréhensive.
JUH SWEEZ kohm-preh-ahn-SEEFF/kohm-preh-ahn-SEEVE.

I feel accepting.
Je suis ouvert/ouverte.
JUH SWEEZ oo-VEHR/oo-VEHRT.

I am peaceful.
Je suis paisible.
JUH SWEEZ peh-ee-ZEEBL.

I feel serene.
Je suis serein/sereine.
JUH SWEEZ suh-REHN/suh-REHN.

I am contented.
Je suis satisfait/satisfaite.
JUH SWEEZ sah-tee-FEH/sah-tee-FEET.

I feel comfortable.
Je suis à l'aise.
JUH SWEEZ ah-lehz.

I am amused.
Je suis amusé/amusée.
JUH SWEEZ ah-moo-ZAY/ah-moo-ZAY.

I feel entertained.
Je suis diverti/divertie.
JUH SWEEZ dee-VEHR-tee/dee-VEHR-tee.

I am surprised.
Je suis surpris/surprise.
JUH SWEEZ soo-PREE/soo-PREEZ.

I feel shocked.
Je suis choqué/choquée.
JUH SWEEZ shoh-KEH/shoh-KEH.

I am disappointed.
Je suis déçu/déçue.
JUH SWEEZ day-SYUH/day-SYUH.

I feel sad.
Je suis triste.
JUH SWEEZ treest.

Many of these phrases are best suited for intermediate speakers, but should also be utilized by beginners to improve your conversations.

I'm feeling great today!
Je me sens très bien aujourd'hui !
Zhuh muh sahN tray byaN oh-zhoor-DWEE!

I've been really tired lately and need to get more sleep.
J'ai été vraiment fatigué(e) dernièrement et j'ai besoin de dormir plus.
Zhay ay-tay vré-mahn fah-tee-GAY dair-nyay-mahn ay zhay buh-ZWAHN duh dohr-MEER ploo.

I need to start exercising more regularly.
Je dois commencer à faire plus d'exercice régulièrement.
Zhuh dwah koh-mahn-SAY ah fair ploo deks-ehr-SEES reh-gyew-lyehr-mahn.

I've been eating healthier and feel much better.
J'ai mangé plus sainement et je me sens beaucoup mieux.
Zhay mahn-zhay ploo say-nuh-mahn ay zhuh muh sahN boh-koo mwah.

I'm trying to cut back on sugar and processed foods.
J'essaie de réduire ma consommation de sucre et de nourriture transformée.
Jess-AY duh ray-DYUR ma kohn-soh-mah-see-YON duh soo-kruh ay duh noo-ree-TOOR trahnz-for-may.

I've been struggling with anxiety and am seeking help.
Je lutte contre l'anxiété et je cherche de l'aide.
Zhuh loot kohn-truh lah-ksyeh-tay ay zhuh shairsh duh lah-eed.

I've been dealing with a lot of stress at work and need to find ways to manage it better.
Je fais face à beaucoup de stress au travail et j'ai besoin de trouver des moyens de mieux le gérer.
Zhuh fay fahs ah boh-koo duh stress oh trav-ah-yay ay zhay buh-ZWAHN duh troo-vay day mwah luh zhay-ray.

I think I'm coming down with a cold.
Je pense que je commence à attraper un rhume.
Zhuh pahns kuh zhuh koh-mahs ah ah-tra-pay uhn room.

I'm recovering from an injury and need to take it easy for a while.
Je me remets d'une blessure et j'ai besoin de prendre du repos pendant un moment.
Zhuh muh ruh-may duhn blah-syur ay zhay buh-ZWAHN duh prahndruh dyuh reh-poh pahN-dahN uhn moh-mahn.

I'm trying to quit smoking for my health.
J'essaie d'arrêter de fumer pour ma santé.
Jess-AY dah-reh-tay duh fyoo-may poor ma sahN-tay.

I've been having trouble sleeping and need to talk to my doctor about it.
J'ai des problèmes de sommeil et j'ai besoin d'en parler à mon médecin.
Zhay day proh-bluhm duh sohm-ay ay zhay buh-ZWAHN dohn pahr-lay ah mohn mayd-sehn.

I've been feeling down lately and think I might be depressed.
Je me sens déprimé(e) ces derniers temps et je pense que je pourrais être déprimé(e).
Zhuh meh SAHN day-pree-may seh DYERN-yay tohN eh zhuh pawns kuh zhuh puh-RRAY day-pray-MAY.

I'm trying to lose weight for my overall health.
J'essaie de perdre du poids pour ma santé générale.
Jess-AY duh pehrdruh dew pwah pour mah sahn-TAY zhen-er-AL.

I've been getting more rest and sleep lately to improve my overall well-being.
J'ai dormi plus et mieux récemment pour améliorer mon bien-être général.
Zhay DOR-mee ploo zay myuh ray-suh-mahn pour ah-mee-lee-or-ay mohn byan-ET-ruh zhen-er-AL.

I'm going to start seeing a therapist to work on my mental health.
Je vais commencer à voir un thérapeute pour travailler sur ma santé mentale.
Zhuh vay komm-ahn-SAY ah vwahng teh-ruh-PUHT poor trah-vee-yay sur mah sahn-TAY mahn-TAL.

I need to go for a check-up with my doctor.
Je dois aller chez mon médecin pour un check-up.
Zhuh dwahz ah-LAY shay mohn may-duh-SAN poor ung check-up.

I'm trying to drink more water and stay hydrated.
J'essaie de boire plus d'eau et de rester hydraté(e).
Jess-AY duh bwah-ruh ploo doh ay-oh et duh reh-stay ee-dra-tay.

I've been experiencing some digestive issues and need to watch what I eat.
J'ai des problèmes de digestion et j'ai besoin de faire attention à ce que je mange.
Zhay day proh-BLEM duh dee-zhe-STEE-yohn eh zhay buh-ZOIN duh fay-ruh ah-tahn-see-yohn ah suh kuh zhuh mahnj.

I'm taking vitamins to supplement my diet.
Je prends des vitamines pour compléter mon régime alimentaire.
Zhuh PRAHNG day VEE-tah-meen poor kohm-play-TAY mohn ray-ZHEEM ahl-ee-mahn-TAIR

I've been feeling more energetic since starting a new exercise routine.
Je me sens plus énergique depuis que j'ai commencé une nouvelle routine d'exercice.
Zhuh muh sahng ploo ZHAY-nair-JEEK duh-PU-ee kuh zhay koh-mahn-SAY ewn noo-VEL roo-TEEN daygz-air-SEES

I'm trying to reduce my alcohol intake for my health.
J'essaie de réduire ma consommation d'alcool pour ma santé.
Zhess-AY duh ray-DUE-re ma kon-so-ma-see-ohn dal-KOOL poor ma sahn-TAY

I'm working on improving my mental clarity and focus.
Je travaille à améliorer ma clarté mentale et ma concentration.
Zhuh trah-vah-yuh ah ah-mey-lee-or-AY ma klaar-TAY mahn-TAHL ay ma kohn-san-tra-see-YON

I need to take a break and relax to reduce my stress levels.
J'ai besoin de prendre une pause et de me détendre pour réduire mon niveau de stress.
Zhay buh-ZWAHN duh PRAHND-run oon PAWS ay duh muh day-tond pour ray-DUE-re mohn niv-oh duh stress

I'm trying to get more fresh fruits and vegetables in my diet.
J'essaie de manger plus de fruits et légumes frais dans mon alimentation.
Zhess-AY duh mahn-JAY plu duh frwee ay lay-gewm fray dahns mohn ahl-ee-man-tay-SYON

I'm feeling more positive and happy since incorporating mindfulness into my daily routine.
Je me sens plus positif et heureux depuis que j'ai intégré la pleine conscience dans ma routine quotidienne.
Zhuh muh sahng ploo po-zee-TEEF ay uhr-UH depuis kuh zhay an-tay-gray la plehn con-see-uhns dahns ma roo-TEEN ko-tee-DYE-EN

How do you stay healthy and fit?
Comment restez-vous en bonne santé et en forme ?
KOH-mahn ruh-STAY voo ahn bohn SANTAY ayn fohm?

Have you been feeling well lately?
Vous sentez-vous bien ces derniers temps ?
Voo sahn-TAY voo byahn sayz DERN-yayr tohn?

Do you have any health concerns you'd like to discuss?
Avez-vous des préoccupations de santé que vous aimeriez discuter ?
AH-veh-voo day PRAY-oh-coo-PAY-syon duh SAN-tay kuh voo
EH-muh-ree-yay dees-kuh-TEY?

Have you been getting enough sleep lately?
Avez-vous suffisamment dormi ces derniers temps ?
AH-veh-voo soo-fiz-AH-mahn DOR-mee sayz DERN-yayr tohn?

Do you follow any particular diet or exercise regimen?
Suivez-vous un régime alimentaire ou un programme d'exercice
particulier ?
Swee-vay-voo uhn ruh-ZHEEM ah-luh-mahn-TAYR oo uhn
proh-GRAMM duhgz-ehr-SEES pahr-tee-kew-LYAY?

How do you manage stress in your life?
Comment gérez-vous le stress dans votre vie ?
KOH-mahn zhuh-RAY voo luh STRESS dahn voh-truh VEE?

Do you take any vitamins or supplements to support your health?
Prenez-vous des vitamines ou des compléments alimentaires pour
soutenir votre santé ?
Pruh-NAY-voo day vee-ta-MEEN oo day kohm-PLAY-mahn
ah-luh-mahn-TAIR pour soo-tuh-NEER vo-truh SAN-tay?

SHOPPING AT A GROCERY STORE

Where can I find the milk?
Où puis-je trouver le lait?
OO pweezh zhuh troo-VAY luh lay

Do you carry almond milk?
Avez-vous du lait d'amande ?
Ah-veh-VOO dew lay dah-MAHND?

Can you direct me to the bread aisle?
Pouvez-vous me diriger vers le rayon du pain?
Poo-VEH-voom duh-ree-JAY vair luh ray-O(N) dew pa(N)?

Where can I find fresh produce?
Où puis-je trouver des produits frais ?
OO pweezh zhuh troo-VAY day proh-dwee freh?

Do you have any ripe bananas?
Avez-vous des bananes mûres ?
Ah-veh-VOO day ba-NAHN myoor?

Where can I find the eggs?
Où puis-je trouver les oeufs ?
OO pweezh zhuh troo-VAY lay zuh?

Do you carry organic produce?
Avez-vous des produits biologiques ?
Ah-veh-VOO day proh-dwee bee-oh-loh-ZHEEK?

Can you direct me to the meat department?
Pouvez-vous me diriger vers le rayon de la viande ?
Poo-veh-VOO muh deer-ee-JAY vair luh ray-OHN duh lah vee-YAND?

Where can I find ground beef?
Où puis-je trouver du boeuf haché ?
OO poo-eezh truh-VAY doo BUHF ah-SHAY?

Do you have any chicken breasts?
Avez-vous des poitrines de poulet ?
Ah-veh-VOO day pwa-TREEN duh poo-LAY?

Can you tell me where the canned goods are located?
Pouvez-vous me dire où se trouvent les conserves ?
Poo-veh-VOO muh deer oo suh troo-VENT lay kon-SERV?

Where can I find the pasta?
Où puis-je trouver les pâtes ?
OO poo-eezh truh-VAY lay PAT

Do you carry gluten-free products?
Avez-vous des produits sans gluten ?
Ah-veh-VOO day proh-DEE-wee sahn gloo-TEN?

Can you direct me to the bakery?
Pouvez-vous me diriger vers la boulangerie ?
Poo-veh-VOO muh deer-ee-JAY vair lah boo-LON-jer-EE?

Where can I find fresh baked bread?
Où puis-je trouver du pain frais ?
OO poo-eezh truh-VAY doo pan fray?

Do you have any bagels left?
Avez-vous encore des bagels ?
Ah-veh-VOO ohn-KOR day BAY-gels?

Can you tell me where the frozen foods are located?
Pouvez-vous me dire où se trouvent les aliments surgelés ?
Poo-VEH-voo muh DEER oo truh-VEUH les ah-lee-MOHN ser-juh-LAY?

Where can I find ice cream?
Où puis-je trouver de la crème glacée ?
Oo PWEEZH truh-VEH duh lah krem GLA-say?

Do you carry any vegan products?
Avez-vous des produits végétaliens ?
Ah-veh-VOO day proh-DWEE veh-zhey-tah-LYEN?

Can you direct me to the deli counter?
Pouvez-vous me diriger vers le comptoir de la charcuterie ?
Poo-VEH-voo muh deer-ee-GAY verr luh kohn-TWAHR duh lah shar-koo-tree?

Where can I find sliced turkey?
Où puis-je trouver de la dinde tranchée ?
Oo PWEEZH truh-VEH duh lah dan-dh trahn-SHAY?

Do you have any freshly made sandwiches?
Avez-vous des sandwiches fraîchement préparés ?
Ah-veh-VOO day sahn-dee-SH frai-SHOM-mohnn pray-pah-RAY?

Can you tell me where the chips and snacks are located?
Pouvez-vous me dire où se trouvent les chips et les snacks ?
Poo-VEH-voo muh DEER oo truh-VEUH lay chips ay lay snaks?

Where can I find potato chips?
Où puis-je trouver des chips de pomme de terre ?
Oo PWEEZH truh-VEH day chips duh pohm duh TAYR?

Do you carry any specialty items such as international foods or spices?
Avez-vous des articles spéciaux comme des aliments ou des épices internationales ?
Ah-veh-VOO day zahr-TEE-kluh speh-see-YOH-kluh kum duh ZAH-lee-mohn oh day eh-PEES eeN-tehr-nah-syoh-NAHL?

Where can I find the rice?
Où puis-je trouver du riz?
Oo pweezh truh-VEH doo REE?

Do you have any quinoa?
Avez-vous du quinoa?
Ah-veh-VOO doo kee-NOH-ah?

Can you direct me to the seafood department?
Pouvez-vous me diriger vers le rayon des fruits de mer?
Poo-veh-VOO muh dee-ree-ZHAY vayr luh ray-AWN day frwee duh mehr?

Where can I find fresh salmon?
Où puis-je trouver du saumon frais?
Oo pweezh truh-VEH doo soh-mohn freh?

Do you carry any sushi-grade fish?
Avez-vous du poisson de qualité sushi ?
Ah-veh-VOO doo pwah-SOHN duh kah-lee-TAY soo-shee?

Can you tell me where the cheese is located?
Pouvez-vous me dire où se trouve le fromage?
Poo-veh-VOO muh DEER oo suh TROOV luh froh-MAZH?

Where can I find cheddar cheese?
Où puis-je trouver du fromage cheddar ?
Oo pweezh truh-VEH doo froh-MAHZH sheh-dahr?

Do you have any goat cheese?
Avez-vous du fromage de chèvre ?
Ah-veh-VOO doo froh-MAHZH duh shev-ruh?

Can you direct me to the bulk foods section?
Pouvez-vous me diriger vers la section des aliments en vrac ?
Poo-VEH-voo muh DEE-ruh-zhay vair lah sek-SYOHN dayz ah-lee-MOHN ah(n) vrahk?

Where can I find nuts and seeds?
Où puis-je trouver des noix et des graines ?
Oo PWEEZH truh-VEH day nwah eh day grahn?

Do you carry any dried fruits?
Avez-vous des fruits secs?
Ah-veh-VOO day frwee SEK?

Can you tell me where the condiments are located?
Pouvez-vous me dire où se trouvent les condiments ?
Poo-VEH-voo muh DEER oo troo-VUH lay kohn-dee-MAHN?

Where can I find ketchup?
Où puis-je trouver du ketchup ?
Oo PWEEZH truh-VEH doo KEH-tchup?

Do you have any mustard?
Avez-vous de la moutarde ?
Ah-veh-VOO duh lah moo-TAHRD?

Can you direct me to the beer and wine section?
Pouvez-vous me diriger vers la section de la bière et du vin ?
Poo-VEH-voo muh DEE-ruh-zhay vair lah sek-SYOHN duh lah byehr eh duh vahn?

Where can I find red wine?
Où puis-je trouver du vin rouge ?
Oo PWEEZH truh-VEH doo vahn roozh?

Do you have any craft beer?
Avez-vous de la bière artisanale ?
AH-veh-VOO duh lah bee-AIR ar-tee-zah-NAL?

Can you tell me where the paper products are located?
Pouvez-vous me dire où se trouvent les produits en papier ?
Poo-VEH-voo muh DEER ooh suh TROO-vuh lay proh-DWEE ahn pah-PYEH?

Where can I find toilet paper?
Où puis-je trouver du papier toilette ?
OO pweezh zhuh troo-VAYr dew pah-PYEH twa-LET?

Do you have any paper towels?
Avez-vous des essuie-tout ?
AH-veh-VOO day zehs-WEH-too?

Can you direct me to the cleaning supplies section?
Pouvez-vous me diriger vers la section des produits de nettoyage ?
Poo-VEH-voo muh deer-ee-GAYr vehr lah seh-KSYON day proh-DWEE duh neh-twah-YAJE?

Where can I find dish soap?
Où puis-je trouver du liquide vaisselle ?
OO pweezh zhuh troo-VAYr dew lee-KEED vay-SELL?

Do you have any laundry detergent?
Avez-vous de la lessive ?
AH-veh-VOO duh lah luh-SEEV?

Can you tell me where the pet food is located?
Pouvez-vous me dire où se trouve la nourriture pour animaux ?
Poo-VEH-voo muh DEER ooh suh TROO-vuh lah noo-ree-TYUR poor ah-nee-MOH?

Where can I find cat food?
Où puis-je trouver de la nourriture pour chats ?
OO pweezh zhuh troo-VAYr duh lah noo-ree-TYUR poor sha?

Can you direct me to the baby products section?
Pouvez-vous me diriger vers la section des produits pour bébés ?
Poo-VEY-voo muh dee-ree-JEY vair lah sek-see-ON day proh-DEE twa BEY-bey?

Where can I find diapers?
Où puis-je trouver des couches ?
Oo pweezh TU-vay day KOO-shuh?

Do you carry any organic baby food?
Avez-vous de la nourriture bio pour bébé ?
Ah-vey-VOO duh lah noo-ree-TOOR bee-oh poor BEY-bey?

Can you tell me where the pharmacy is located?
Pouvez-vous me dire où se trouve la pharmacie ?
Poo-VEY-voo muh deer oo suh TROOV lah fahr-mah-SEE?

Where can I find pain relievers?
Où puis-je trouver des analgésiques ?
Oo pweezh TU-vay day an-al-jey-ZEEK?

Do you carry any cough medicine?
Avez-vous des médicaments contre la toux ?
Ah-vey-VOO day may-dee-ka-mahn kohn-truh lah too?

Can you direct me to the cosmetics aisle?
Pouvez-vous me diriger vers le rayon des cosmétiques ?
Poo-VEY-voo muh dee-ree-JEY vair luh ray-on day koz-MEH-tiks?

Where can I find shampoo?
Où puis-je trouver du shampooing ?
Oo pweezh TU-vay duh sham-pwahn?

Do you carry any natural or organic beauty products?
Avez-vous des produits de beauté naturels ou biologiques ?
AH-vay voo day proh-DWEE duh bo-TAY na-tyuh-REL ooh bee-oh-loh-ZHEEK?

Can you tell me where the kitchenware is located?
Pouvez-vous me dire où se trouve la vaisselle ?
Poo-VAY voo muh DEER ooh suh TROOV la vay-ZELL?

Where can I find pots and pans?
Où puis-je trouver des casseroles et des poêles ?
OO pwissh zhuh troo-VAY day kass-uh-ROLL ay day pwell?

Do you carry any baking supplies?
Avez-vous des ustensiles de pâtisserie ?
AH-vay voo day yoo-stahn-SEEL duh pah-tee-SEE-ree?

Can you direct me to the electronics section?
Pouvez-vous m'indiquer où se trouve le rayon électronique ?
Poo-VAY voo man-dee-KEY oo suh TROOV luh ray-OHN ay-lehk-troh-NEEK?

Where can I find headphones?
Où puis-je trouver des écouteurs ?
OO pwissh zhuh troo-VAY day ay-koo-TUHR?

Do you carry any phone chargers?
Avez-vous des chargeurs de téléphone ?
AH-vay voo day shar-ZHUHR duh tay-lay-FOHN?

Can you tell me where the office supplies are located?
Pouvez-vous me dire où se trouvent les fournitures de bureau ?
Poo-VAY voo muh DEER oo suh TROOV lay foo-ni-TYOOR duh boo-ROH?

GIVING AND RECEIVING INSTRUCTIONS

Here's what you need to do.
Voici ce que vous devez faire.
Vwah-SEE suh kuh voo DUH-vay fair.

Let me show you how to do it.
Laissez-moi vous montrer comment le faire.
LEH-say mwah voo mohn-TRAY koh-MOHN luh fair.

It's simple, just follow these steps.
C'est simple, il suffit de suivre ces étapes.
SEH seeM-pluh, eel soo-fee duh swee-vruh sayz EY-tap.

Start by doing this.
Commencez par faire ceci.
Koh-MON-say par fair suh-SEE.

Next, you'll want to...
Ensuite, vous voudrez...
Ahn-SUHT, voo voo-DREH...

The first thing you should do is...
La première chose que vous devriez faire est de...
Lah PREH-myer shohz kuh voo duh-VREH fair EH duh...

Don't forget to...
N'oubliez pas de...
Noo-blee-yeh pah duh...

Make sure to...
Assurez-vous de...
Ah-syuh-RAY voo duh...

You'll need to...
Vous devrez...
Voo duh-VREH...

Begin by...
Commencez par...
Koh-MON-say par...

Follow these steps...
Suivez ces étapes...
Swee-vay sayz EY-tap...

Take your time and...
Prenez votre temps et...
Pruh-NAY voh-truh tahn eh...

Be sure to...
Assurez-vous de...
Ah-syuh-RAY voo duh...

Remember to...
N'oubliez pas de...
Noo-blee-yeh pah duh...

Double-check that...
Vérifiez deux fois que...
Vay-ree-FEE-yeh deuh FWAH kuh...

Let me know if you have any questions.
Faites-moi savoir si vous avez des questions.
Fet-mwah sav-WAH-ree si vooz ah-VAY day kehs-TYOHN.

If you get stuck, try...
Si vous êtes coincé, essayez...
Si vooz EH-tay kwahn-SAY, eh-seh-YEH...

Remember, practice makes perfect.
Rappelez-vous, la pratique rend parfait.
Ra-puh-lay-voo, lah pree-TEEK rahn par-FEH.

You'll get the hang of it in no time.
Vous prendrez le coup en un rien de temps.
Voo prahn-DREH luh koo ahn uhn RYAHN duh tah.

Trust me, it's not as hard as it looks.
Croyez-moi, ce n'est pas aussi difficile que ça en a l'air.
Kruh-YEH mwah, suh neh pah zoh-SEE dee-fee-SEEL kuh sah ah lehr.

That makes sense.
Ça a du sens.
Sah ah dew sahns.

I think I can handle that.
Je pense que je peux m'en occuper.
Zhuh pahns kuh zhuh puh mohn ohk-yuh-PAY.

Great, thanks for explaining it.
Génial, merci de l'explication.
Zhay-nee-AHL, mehr-see duh lek-spee-kah-see-YOHN.

I'll give it a try.
Je vais essayer.
Zhuh vay ess-eh-YAY.

Got it, thanks for your help.
Compris, merci pour votre aide.
Kohm-PREE, mehr-see poor vo-truh ohd.

I appreciate your guidance.
J'apprécie votre guidage.
Zhap-preh-SEE vo-truh gee-dazh.

This is very helpful, thanks.
C'est très utile, merci.
Seh tray yoo-TEEL, mehr-see.

I think I'm ready to do it now.
Je pense que je suis prêt à le faire maintenant.
Zhuh pahns kuh zhuh swee PRET ah luh fair main-ten-ahn.

I'll make sure to do that.
Je vais m'assurer de faire cela.
Zhuh vay mah-seh-RAY duh fair suh-LAH.

Okay, I'll keep that in mind.
D'accord, je vais m'en souvenir.
Dah-KOR, zhuh vay mahn soo-ve-NIHR.

Take a moment to...
Prenez un moment pour...
Pre-NAY uh mo-MAHN poor...

Keep in mind that...
Gardez à l'esprit que...
Gar-DAY ah leh-SPREH keuh..
.

Start off by...
Commencez par...
Ko-MON-say pahr...

Before you do anything else...
Avant de faire quoi que ce soit d'autre...
Ah-VAHN duh fair kwah kuh swah-tuh DOR...

Be careful to...
Soyez prudent pour...
Swah-YAY proo-DAHN poor...

Okay, got it.
D'accord, compris.
Dah-KOR, kohn-PREE.

I understand what you're saying.
Je comprends ce que vous dites.
Zhuh kohn-PRAHN suh kuh voo DEET.

Can you explain that again?
Pouvez-vous expliquer cela à nouveau ?
Poo-VAY voo ek-spee-KAY sah-LAH ah noo-VOH.

Sorry, I didn't catch that.
Désolé, je n'ai pas compris.
Day-zoh-LAY, zhuh neh pah kohn-PREE.

Could you repeat the last step?
Pouvez-vous répéter la dernière étape ?
Poo-VAY voo ray-PAY-tay lah dayR-NYAYR ay-TAP.

I'm not sure I understand.
Je ne suis pas sûr de comprendre.
Zhuh nuh swee pah soor duh kohn-PRAHND-ruh.

So, I just need to...
Donc, j'ai juste besoin de...
Dohnk, zhay joo-stuh buh-ZWAHN duh...

Is there anything else I need to know?
Y a-t-il autre chose que je dois savoir ?
Ee ah-teel OH-truh shohz kuh zhuh dwah sah-VWAHR.

Thanks for your help.
Merci pour votre aide.
Mehr-see poor vo-truh ohd.

I'll get right on it.
Je vais m'en occuper tout de suite.
Zhuh vay mohn ohk-yuh-PAY too duh SWEEHT.

EXPRESSING UNCERTAINTY AND PROBABILITY

I'm not entirely sure.
Je ne suis pas tout à fait sûre.
Zheuh nuh swee pah too tah FAY syur

It could be possible.
C'est possible.
SEH poh-SEE-bl

I'm not convinced yet.
Je ne suis pas convaincue encore.
Zheuh nuh swee pah kohn-VAH-kyuh ahn-KOR

It's hard to say.
C'est difficile à dire.
SEH dee-fee-SEEL ah DEER

Maybe, but maybe not.
Peut-être, mais peut-être pas.
PUHT-ETR, may PUHT-ETR pah

I'm not completely confident.
Je ne suis pas complètement confiante.
Zheuh nuh swee pah kohm-PLYEH-mahn kohn-fee-AHN

There's a chance that...
Il y a une chance que...
Eel yah ewn SHAHNS kuh...

It's a toss-up.
C'est un pari.
SEH tahn-TAY

It's anyone's guess.
C'est la devinette de tout le monde.
SEH lah duh-vee-NEHT duh too leuh-MOND

I'm on the fence about it.
Je suis indécise à ce sujet.
Zheuh swee zehn-deh-SEE ah suh suh-ZHAY

I'm not entirely convinced.
Je ne suis pas tout à fait convaincue.
Zheuh nuh swee pah too tah FAY kohn-VAH-kyuh

It's possible, but unlikely.
C'est possible, mais peu probable.
SEH poh-SEE-bl, may peuh PROH-bahbl

It's probable, but not certain.
C'est probable, mais pas certain.
SEH PROH-bahbl, may pah sehr-TEN

It's up in the air.
C'est incertain.
SEH ahn-SEHR-TEN

It's a bit of a mystery.
C'est un mystère.
SEH uh MISS-tehr

I'm not sure, but it's worth exploring.
Je ne suis pas sûre, mais ça vaut la peine d'explorer.
Zheuh nuh swee pah SYUR, may sah voh lah PEH-nuh deks-ploh-RAY

There's a slim chance.
Il y a une faible chance.
Eel yah ewn FAYBL SHAHNS

It's not out of the question.
Ce n'est pas hors de question.
Suh neh pah ohr duh kuh-STYON

It's not very likely.
Ce n'est pas très probable.
Suh neh pah tray proh-BAHBL

It's a long shot.
C'est une chance très mince.
SEH tun SHAHNS tray mahnss

It's possible, but I wouldn't bet on it.
C'est possible, mais je ne parierais pas là-dessus.
SEH poh-SEE-bl, may nuh pah-reeh-RAY pah lah-DEH-SU

It's hard to determine.
C'est difficile à déterminer.
SEH dee-fee-SEEL ah day-tayr-mee-NAY

It's uncertain.
C'est incertain.
SEH ahn-SEHR-TEN

It's a 50-50 chance.
C'est une chance de 50-50.
SEH tun SHAHNS duh SANK-awnk-SANK-awnk

It's a matter of perspective.
C'est une question de point de vue.
SEH tun keh-styon duh pwahn duh VOO

It's open to interpretation.
C'est ouvert à l'interprétation.
SEH oo-VEHR ah lahn-tehr-preh-tah-see-YAWN

I can't say for sure.
Je ne peux pas dire avec certitude.
Zheuh nuh pu pah DEER ah-vehk sehr-tee-TOOD

It's a possibility, but not a certainty.
C'est une possibilité, mais pas une certitude.
SEH tun poh-see-BEE-li-TAY, may pahzewn ser-tee-TOOD

It's a grey area.
C'est un domaine gris.
SEH tun doh-MEN grEE

It's unclear.
C'est flou.
SEH floo

It's a matter of probability.
C'est une question de probabilité.
SEH tun keh-styon duh proh-bah-bee-LAY-tee

It's debatable.
C'est sujet à débat.
SEH soo-ZHEH ah day-BAH

It's subjective.
C'est subjectif.
SEH sub-jek-TEEF

It's not beyond the realm of possibility.
Ce n'est pas hors de portée.
Suh neh pah ohr duh pohr-TAY

It's conceivable.
C'est envisageable.
SEH ahn-vee-za-JAH-bl

It's a matter of opinion.
C'est une question d'opinion.
SEH tun keh-styon dah-pee-NYAWN

It's not impossible.
Ce n'est pas impossible.
Suh neh pahz-awn-SEE-bluh

It's not a sure thing.
Ce n'est pas certain.
Suh neh pah sehr-TEHN

It's not guaranteed.
Ce n'est pas garanti.
Suh neh pah gah-RAHN-tee

It's not definitive.
Ce n'est pas définitif.
Suh neh pah day-fee-NEE-tee

Printed in Great Britain
by Amazon